A Time with Our Children
Year B

A Time with Our Children
Stories for Use in Worship

Year B

Dianne E. Deming

United Church Press
Cleveland, Ohio

United Church Press, Cleveland, Ohio 44115
© 1993 by Dianne E. Deming

Biblical quotations, unless otherwise noted, are from the New Revised
Standard Version of the Bible, © 1989 by the Division of Christian Edu-
cation of the National Council of the Churches of Christ in the U.S.A.,
and are used by permission

Illustrations by Carin Shanley

Printed in the United States of America
The paper used in this publication is acid free and meets the minimum
requirements of American National Standard for Information Sciences-
Permanence of Paper for Printed Library Materials, ANSI Z39.48-1984

98 97 96 95 94 93   5 4 3 2 1

Library of Congress Cataloging-in-Publication Data
(Revised for volume 2)

Deming, Dianne E.
    A time with our children.
    Includes indexes.
    Contents: [1] Year A — [2] Year B.
    1. Children's sermons. 2. Church year sermons. I. Title.
BV4315.D422   1992
252'.53   92-31638
    ISBN 0-8298-0941-4 (Year A : alk. paper)
    ISBN 0-8298-0952-X (Year B : alk. paper)

To
Leonard and Anne Jones
Dennis and Kathy Onnen
with love

Contents

Acknowledgments

With the completion of this book, I also finish the three-volume series of children's sermons, *A Time with Our Children: Stories for Use in Worship*. This effort would never have gotten to this point of satisfying conclusion were it not for the grace of God, the love of the project, and the support of family, friends, and colleagues.

To my family and close friends whose interest and encouragement kept me going—thank you. To all who have bought and used the books—thank you, and I'm glad you found them helpful. To my mom, Anne B. Jones, and my friend, Sarah Rinehimer—thank you for typing the manuscript. Thanks go to Carin Shanley for her artwork, and to Lisa Motz-Storey, Robert Zanicky, and Frank Deming for lending me story ideas.

Thank you to Richard Brown, Marjorie Pon, and everyone at the press who made this series possible.

And finally, once again I must thank all the children in my life, especially Scott and John, for helping me remember what it's like to be a child.

Introduction

Families are busier today than they have ever been, and one reason is that children today are involved in so many activities. One of my difficulties as a youth leader was finding enough free time in the young people's over-scheduled lives. The age at which formal activities—sports, lessons, scouts, and so on—threaten to take over a child's week is inching downward. This realization puts the children's sermon in a unique perspective. The storyteller is given a rare gift—the gift of five to ten minutes of the child's undivided time and attention.

It is up to us as church leaders to make that gift worth the giving. To accomplish this goal, we must keep several objectives in mind.

1. Be sure that the children's sermons are for the children. The stories should relate the gospel in ways a child can understand, finding places where God's Word intersects with a child's life experience and using words and images with which a child is familiar.

2. The storyteller must always respect his or her audience and not set the children up to be embarrassed or laughed at for the amusement of the adults. Laughter is great, as long as it is *with* the children, not *at* them.

3. During their special time, the children should gain an understanding that they are loved and cared for by their God and their church. This is perhaps the greatest benefit they derive from this experience.

4. Having a children's sermon during the course of worship does not mean that the rest of the service needn't have some significance for the younger members of the congregation. Five minutes of quality time does not let worship planners off the hook for the other fifty-five minutes. The entire congregation needs to be considered in composing the whole worship experience.

Time is one of the most valuable commodities we have today. The stories in this book have been written to make the most of the gift of time with your children. May God bless you in this important ministry.

How to Use this Book

The stories in the book are based on the scripture readings from the *Revised Common Lectionary* (Year B). There are also topical and scriptural indexes for those who do not follow the lectionary.

Several of the stories call for the use of a flannel board and flannel-board figures. These figures, with instructions on how to prepare them and the board, are found in the Appendix.

Finally, I encourage you to take these stories and make them your own. Where specific towns, churches, locations, or people are named by way of example, fill in with details that fit your own situation. But even more than that, tell the stories in your own words, add personal anecdotes to enhance your message, and change the stories in any way that will make them more effective for you. Have fun, and may God be with you.

Season of Advent

Counting the Days until Christmas

Props and Preparation Needed

Advent chains—paper chains with one link for each day in Advent. Count up the days in the Advent season this year (twenty-seven for 1993) and divide that number by two, rounding up to the next whole number (fourteen). Draw thirteen lines across an 8½-by-11-inch piece of paper, making fourteen sections. Do the same to a second sheet of paper, then label the sections for the days in Advent, using one page for the even-numbered days and the other for the odd-numbered days. On each day's strip, write or type an Advent message. Sunday messages could be appropriate Scripture readings, and other days could include such messages as "Give someone you know a hug" or "Make Christmas cookies and share them." You could also include reminders for church events such as "Attend Westminster's Advent Workshop." Photocopy the first page onto red construction paper and the second onto green, making enough copies for all the children. Cut apart one set of strips, and glue together a paper chain, making sure the days are in proper order

The Message

Good morning, boys and girls. Does anybody know what day today is? (*Listen to answers.*) Today is the first Sunday in Advent, right. How did you know that? (*Listen to answers.*) You noticed the Advent wreath over there and the Christmas decorations. That's good. The first Sunday in Advent means that Christmas is only four short weeks away—twenty-seven days, to be exact. Actually, twenty-seven days can be a long time to wait for something, especially something as special as Christmas.

I have something for you that might make the waiting a little bit easier. It will give you some interesting things to do while you're waiting and let you know when you're getting close to Christmas. It's called an Advent chain. (*Show your chain.*)

There is one link in the chain for every day between now and Christmas. That's one link for every day during the season of Advent. Each link has a message on it for that day. Every day, starting today, I will tear one link off the chain and read the message. Chelsea, would you please tear today's link off the chain for me? (*Have a child help you, then read the message.*) Today's message says, "Read Isaiah 9:2, 6–7." Let's read that passage now. (*Read the Scripture.*)

God's people, the Hebrews, waited thousands of years for God to send them this special person, the One who would be called "Wonderful Counselor, Mighty God, Everlasting Father, Prince of Peace." That person finally came to Earth as a tiny baby born in Bethlehem. His name was Jesus. It is Jesus' birthday that we celebrate on Christmas.

We don't have to wait thousands of years to celebrate God's gift to us in Jesus, but we do have to wait twenty-seven days for Jesus' birthday. I have an Advent chain for each of you to make at home. (*Pass out the sheets.*) Cut the strips on the sheets apart and glue the links together. You might need some help making sure the days are in order. Each day, tear off one link, read the message, and follow its instructions if you can. As the chain gets shorter, you'll know you're getting closer to Christmas. When all the links are gone, the waiting will be over, and the very next day will be Jesus' birthday.

Let's Pray. Dear God, sometimes we are not very good at waiting. Thank you for giving us such a special day to look forward to, and such a wonderful event to celebrate—the birth of Jesus. We pray in Jesus' name. Amen.

Planning Ahead

Look at the preparation needed for next Sunday's story. You may want to enlist the help of a craftsperson.

A Soft, Loving Place

Props and Preparation Needed

One plastic sandwich bag containing thirty one-inch pieces of yellow yarn for each child

One popsicle-stick manger for each child. To construct each manger, glue two popsicle sticks (sold in craft stores) together to make two Xs. (A hot glue gun works best, but extra tacky craft glue will do.) These are the supports for the manger. Hold two Xs, one in front of the other and three to four inches apart. Glue additional sticks horizontally across the top half of the supports, starting where the Xs intersect. Glue sticks up the sides until you reach the tops of the support sticks. Congratulations, you have built a manger! (Or cut a toilet paper tube in half so that you have two shorter tubes, then cut each of these two tubes in half lengthwise. This will give you four curved pieces of cardboard—four mangers.)

The Message

Today is the second Sunday in Advent already. Who remembers what Advent is? (*Listen to answers.*) Advent is the four-week period before Christmas. Since this is the second Sunday in Advent, that means Christmas is only three weeks away.

Advent is a very busy time. Most of us spend Advent getting ready for Christmas. There's a lot to do, isn't there? What are some of the things you and your family are doing this Advent to get ready for Christmas? (*Listen to answers*). Yes, it sounds like you are all very busy, helping to get your homes ready for Christmas and preparing special food and gifts. There's one other thing we need to do this Advent to get ready for Christmas. We all need to prepare our hearts to welcome Jesus. We can do this in many ways. Each time we remember that Christmas is special because it is Jesus' birthday, we are getting our hearts ready in welcome. You might want to ask your mom or dad to read you the story of Jesus' birth for your bedtime story sometime during Advent.

When we talk to God in prayer, we help prepare our hearts for Christmas. And when we do kind things for others, we are getting our hearts ready to welcome Jesus. You can do chores for your parents, clean up your toys without being asked, help carry things in from the car, or set the table for dinner. When you're shopping for gifts for the people on your list, you might buy an extra toy and donate it to Toys for Tots, to help make another child's Christmas happier. You and your family could also donate food to a food bank, to be shared with people who don't have enough. You could shovel your neighbor's sidewalk or take her dog for a walk. Every time we do something kind or generous for another person, we help prepare our hearts for Christmas.

When Jesus was born, Mary wrapped him up and put him in a manger filled with soft hay. It made a pretty nice bed for the new baby. I have a little manger for you today. (*Pass out mangers.*) The only problem is that it doesn't have any hay in it. It would make an awfully hard bed for the baby Jesus. So I'm also going to give you some hay. (*Pass out bags of yarn.*) Each time you listen to the Christmas story from the Bible, or say a prayer, or do a kind deed for someone, put one piece of hay into the manger. As you prepare your manger to receive the baby Jesus by filling it with soft hay, you will be preparing your heart, too, by filling it with love. When you come to church on Christmas Eve, I will have a baby Jesus for each of you to put in your manger, and I hope he will have a soft, loving place to sleep.

Let's Pray. Dear God, Advent is such a hectic time. While we are busy getting everything else ready for Christmas, don't let us forget to prepare our hearts. In the name of Jesus, whose birthday we celebrate, Amen.

Christmas Wishes

Props Needed
  A Christmas wish list

The Message
  Good morning, girls and boys. Christmas is on its way. Are your Advent chains getting shorter? They should be about half gone now. There are only two weeks left until Christmas. Have you given any thought to what you hope Santa will bring you? What are some of the things you would like to find under your Christmas trees? (*Listen to answers.*) Wow—that's some pretty neat stuff!
  I brought a Christmas list to share with you this morning. Let me read it to you: "A new bike, a red sweater, an electric can opener, a puppy, world peace, an end to air pollution, and no more lying in the world."
  Do you think Santa would be able to bring me all the things on my list? What things would Santa be able to bring? (*Listen to answers.*) What things on my list would Santa not be able to deliver? (*Pause.*)
  Have you ever hoped for something that you didn't get for Christmas? Santa can't always give us everything we want, can he? Sometimes the things we hope for may be impractical—too big or too expensive, like a pony. I know many children wish that Santa would bring them ponies for Christmas, but very few children have a place big enough to keep a pony. Maybe what you hope for is too dangerous or in some other way wouldn't be right for you, like a toy you're not old enough for yet. Sometimes children ask Santa to make things happen, like making a sick friend well, or bringing parents back together after a divorce. But these are things that Santa simply does not have the power to do. And then, other times, we hope for something really, really hard. We run to the tree when its time to unwrap gifts, and there's the very thing we dreamed of—a new bike, or a doll, or a pair of roller

skates. We look toward the chimney or up at the top of the tree and whisper, "Thank you, Santa."

The people of Israel—God's people—had hoped and hoped and hoped for thousands of years. They weren't hoping for toys or games, and Santa wasn't around yet. There wasn't even Christmas because this was before Jesus was born. The people of Israel hoped and prayed to God to help them, and God promised to send them a special leader who would make their lives better. God called that leader the Messiah. Every year the people hoped and prayed that this would be the year the Messiah would come.

Finally, when the time was right, God answered the people's prayers and sent the Messiah to them. Most people didn't recognize their leader at first, but a few did. Mary and Joseph knew before Jesus was born that God had important plans for their baby. Some shepherds heard about the birth and went to see Jesus right away. They understood that this baby was special. Some wise men traveled all the way from a foreign country to worship the new leader because they knew that this was no ordinary child.

We know that Mary, Joseph, the shepherds, and the wise men were right. The baby they all watched and worshipped and loved was sent from God to help God's people in all places and in all times. Jesus was the one the people had hoped would come to make their lives better. We recognize Jesus as our Messiah, too.

Jesus is called the "hope of the world." This means that Jesus can make the world a better place. One way he does this is by helping all of us to be kinder, more loving, more generous, less selfish, and fairer toward others. Jesus is our hope and the answer to our prayers.

Let's Pray. Dear God, thank you for answering the prayers of your people by sending us this special leader to help us become the best people we can be. In Jesus' name, we pray. Amen.

Luke 1:26–38

Christmas Surprises

Prop Needed
A jack-in-the-box

The Message

Good morning, girls and boys. This morning I brought something to show you from my friend Joey's toy box. (*Show the jack-in-the-box.*) It doesn't take any batteries, and it doesn't need to be plugged in, but it does something really neat. Let me show you. (*Turn the handle until jack pops out of the box.*) Isn't that fun? How many of you were surprised when the clown popped out of the box? Raise your hands. Only two of you? If you were not surprised when the clown popped out of the box, raise your hand. Why weren't you big kids surprised? (*Pause for answers.*) Oh, you've seen a jack-in-the-box before. You knew what to expect, didn't you? Since you had seen a toy like this before, you knew that when I turned the handle, something would pop out of the top, so you weren't surprised when the clown popped out. That makes sense.

What about the very first time you ever saw a jack-in-the-box? I'll bet you were very young, maybe even a baby. You were probably surprised by the clown popping out the very first time you ever watched someone turn the crank of a jack-in-the-box, weren't you? I'm sure I was.

What about the first time you saw a turtle pull its head and legs into its shell? Do you think that surprised you? Or what about the first time you ate ice cream? Babies get real funny looks on their faces the first time they eat ice cream because they're surprised by how cold it is. Have any of you ever touched a snake? Were you surprised by how the snake's skin felt? Why? (*Listen to answers.*) Most people expect snakes to feel slimy, but their skin is dry, isn't it?

These things that were surprises the first time you experienced them—watching a turtle, tasting ice cream, or feeling a snake—are you surprised by them any more? Every time you eat ice cream, are you surprised by how cold it is? No, you know how it's going to feel before you put it into your mouth because you've eaten ice cream before.

It's the same way with lots of things in our lives. The first time we see or do something new, it's surprising. But after we've done it or seen it a few times, we're not surprised anymore. The event can still be fun—ice cream still tastes good and turtles are still interesting to watch—but we aren't surprised by them anymore.

Believe it or not, the same thing can happen to Christmas if we let it. Imagine how surprised Mary and Joseph must have been when an angel came from God to tell them they were going to have a very special baby. Imagine how surprised the shepherds must have been when they were minding their own business, watching their sheep, and an angel told them about the baby Jesus. Imagine how surprised the wise men must have been to find the new king born in a barn full of animals and straw.

Even though we have heard the story many times, Christmas does not have to lose its surprises. God sent Jesus into the world because God loves each of us more than we will ever be able to understand. God's love for us keeps on surprising us every day, every week, and every year. Christmas is full of surprises, no matter how many times we hear the story, and I don't only mean what's inside the wrapped packages under the tree. God shows us love in surprising new ways all the time—when someone gives you an unexpected smile, helps you with a project, or reads you an extra story. When you offer to set the table, clean your room, or share a toy with your brother or sister, you are showing God's love to others.

The angel told Mary, "For nothing will be impossible with God." If we expect the impossible, this Christmas and every day will be filled with wonderful surprises.

Let's Pray. Dear God, you surprise us with your love at Christmas and throughout the year. Help us to share that surprising love with others. In Jesus' name. Amen.

Season of Christmas

Luke 2:1–20
Matthew 2:1–12

Called to the Manger

Props and Preparation Needed

A nativity scene, complete with holy family, shepherds, wise men, angel, animals, stable, and a star (a Christmas ornament, cookie cutter, posterboard on a stick—whatever you can come up with). On the communion table or in some other central place, set up crèche with stable, Mary, Joseph, Jesus, and the animals. Place shepherds and sheep several yards away, such as on top of the piano. Put the wise men and their camels way back in the narthex. Have an usher ready to help the children in the narthex if necessary. Storyteller should have the angel and the star concealed but readily accessible

A peanut baby Jesus for each child, as promised on the second Sunday in Advent. To make a baby Jesus, wrap a peanut with cotton gauze, leaving a space exposed for the face. Secure the gauze with a rubber band. Draw eyes, nose, and a mouth on the face with a pen

The Message

Who can tell me what day it is today? (*Pause.*) That means tomorrow is what? Christmas, that's right! Christmas is the birthday of a very special person, isn't it? I'd like to have all of you help me tell the story of Jesus' birth right now. Will you do that for me? Good.

Mary and Joseph were two Jewish people who lived in a city called Nazareth. Joseph worked as a carpenter, building things out of wood. Mary was going to have a baby very soon. They were very happy together and looking forward to the birth of their first child.

Then they heard some bad news. All Jewish people had to travel to the town where the husband in the family was born so the government could count everybody. The Romans who were in charge wanted to make sure that they weren't missing anybody who should be paying taxes. The news was bad for Mary and Joseph because Mary was so close to having her baby, and the trip would be hard for her. Remember, there were no cars or buses in those days. She would have to walk or ride on a donkey.

When they finally arrived in Joseph's home town of Bethlehem, Mary and Joseph heard more bad news. All the hotels were full. But a kind innkeeper saw how badly Mary and Joseph needed a place to stay, so he offered them his stable.

That night Mary had her baby. She and Joseph named the baby Jesus. The animals in the stable watched the little one sleep. Mary and Joseph knew that their baby was special because an angel sent from God had told them he would be. God wanted other people to know that Jesus had been born too, so God sent angels out to spread the good news.

Do you remember whom the angels went to see? (*Pause for answers.*) The shepherds, that's right. The shepherds were watching their sheep just like they did every night. They were just outside of town and not very far from the stable where Joseph and Mary and the new baby were. All of a sudden, an angel appeared and said to them, "Do not be afraid; for see—I am bringing you good news of great joy for all the people: to you is born this day in the city of David . . . a Messiah, the Lord" (Luke 2:10–11). Then the night sky was filled with angels singing praises to God.

Does anyone see the shepherds we need for our nativity scene? They aren't very far away. (*Wait while the children look around.*) Yes, there they are over on the piano. John, you take this angel, and all of you go with him. Pretend you are God's angels, and bring the shepherds to the stable to see Jesus. That's what the shepherds did after the angels delivered God's message to them. They came to see the baby for themselves.

(*After group reassembles and shepherds have been placed on crèche, continue.*) So the shepherds heard the good news of Jesus' birth from the angels. And there was another group who came to visit the baby Jesus. Who were they? (*Pause.*) How did the wise men learn that Jesus had been born? (*Pause.*) They saw a new star in the sky and believed this meant a king had been born. Did the wise men come from close by or from far away? (*Pause.*) Far away, that's right. They lived not only in a different town but even in a different country from where Jesus and Mary and Joseph were. The wise men followed that new star until they found Jesus.

Where do you think the wise men for our nativity scene might be waiting? Where is the farthest away spot in our sanctuary?

(*Pause.*) The place where you come in, that's right. Paige, you lead the group back to the narthex, carrying the star. Hold it way up high so the wise men can see it. The ushers in the back will help all of you with the wise men, and you bring them to the stable where we'll set them up.

(*When the children have returned and the wise men are in place, continue.*) The shepherds didn't have to come very far to get to the stable. The wise men made a long journey from a faraway land before they finally arrived. But whether they came from near or far, all of these people came for the same reason. And it's the same reason we gather in worship this evening—to meet the special baby God sent to save the world.

Let's Pray. Dear God, the day we have waited for so long is finally here. Thank you for sending Jesus into the world as a little baby. Thank you for the miracle of Christmas. Amen.

(*Give each child a peanut baby Jesus, reminding them of the story from the second Sunday in Advent.*)

Hopes and Dreams

Props and Preparation Needed
Pictures of infants, cut from magazines and mounted on construction paper or recycled file folders

The Message
I have several pictures to show you, and I'd like you to tell me what they have in common. In what way are these pictures all the same? (*Show pictures and listen to children's answers.*) These are all pictures of babies, that's right. And the babies in these pictures have something in common with each of you, too. Their parents love them and want the very best for them as they grow up. I know that your parents love you and only want the very best for you, too.

Parents want their children to be happy and healthy, to have enough food to eat and nice friends to play with. They want their kids to learn to be responsible, honest, and fair to others. Some parents want their children to become doctors or teachers. Others want them to take over a family business when they grow up. Some parents dream of their children becoming famous movie stars or football players or concert pianists. Other parents simply hope that their children will have enough food to eat each day.

All parents have hopes and dreams for their children. One hope that all the parents in this room share is that our children will be faithful followers of Jesus all their lives. When a baby is brought to church to be baptized (or dedicated), the parents are showing God and the congregation that they want their child to know and love Jesus and to be a part of the church always.

When Jesus was a baby, Mary and Joseph had hopes and dreams too. God's angel had promised them that their baby would be special, but they didn't know in what way. Mary and Joseph were people of the Jewish faith, and they wanted Jesus to be a strong member of their religion also. The Jewish people have special ways of welcoming babies into their religion, just as we have baptism. So Jesus' parents took him to the temple in Jerusalem when he was eight days old to present him to God and the congregation.

At the temple, Jesus was circumcised and officially given his name. Mary and Joseph named him Jesus because that was the name the angel of God had told them to use. Jesus is a Greek word for the Hebrew name Joshua. It's the same name as Joshua, only in a different language. It means "the Lord is salvation." Since Jesus was their first child, Joseph and Mary also paid an offering of five sheckels.

When Mary and Joseph brought Jesus to the temple, they met a very old man there named Simeon. Simeon took Jesus in his arms, held the tiny baby, and prayed to God. He said, "Master, you are now letting me, your servant, die in peace, just like you promised; because I have seen the one you sent to save the world; he will teach all people about your love, and share your glory with your people, Israel."

Mary and Joseph were amazed at what Simeon said about their little baby—that God had sent Jesus to save the world. Then Simeon blessed them and said to Mary, "This child will cause a lot of change in Israel. Some people will be against him— and you will suffer a great deal of pain, too."

A woman named Anna then saw Jesus. She began praising God and telling everyone about the child God had sent to help the people.

Mary still didn't understand what plans God had for Jesus, and Simeon's warning may have worried her. No parent wants to be told that her child will have enemies and that she will also have pain. But I'm sure Mary realized that worrying too much wouldn't do any good. She and Joseph went home to Nazareth where Jesus grew and became strong and wise and a faithful servant of God.

Let's Pray. Dear God, help us all become strong and wise and your faithful servants. Amen.

Epiphany and the Season Following

Rejoice

Second Chances

Props Needed

An assortment of New Year's Eve party supplies—hats, noise-makers, horns

The Message

Yesterday was a very special day. Can anyone tell me what day it was yesterday? January first, New Year's Day, that's right. It was the first day of a brand new year. Two days ago we were still in the year 1993, and then at midnight on Friday night, the year changed to 1994.

Lots of people make a big deal about the new year. Did any of you go to a New Year's Eve party? Did your parents go and leave you home with a babysitter? Many times New Year's Eve parties are just for grownups because the whole point of the party is to stay up really late. Then, at midnight, when the old year is over and the new year begins, everyone shouts "Happy New Year" and makes lots of noise with horns and noisemakers like these. (*Bring out hats and noisemakers.*)

Since some of us didn't go to a party this year, let's pretend that it's New Year's Eve right now. We'll pretend that it's one minute to midnight. Everybody put on a hat and take a horn or noise-maker, but don't make any noise with them yet. (*Look at your watch.*) It's getting close to midnight now. When there are only ten seconds left, we'll all count down from ten, like when the space shuttle is getting ready to take off. Then, when we're done counting, everyone shout "Happy New Year" and sound your horns and noisemakers. Everybody ready? (*Look at your watch.*) Fifteen seconds. Help me count now. (*Count down.*) Happy New Year! Very good.

There are other special ways that people celebrate the new year. There are parades and important football games on television. Most people have the day off from work, and there isn't any school either, even when January first is a weekday.

People make a big deal about the new year because they feel it is a chance to start over. If someone has had bad things happen to her in the old year—like losing a job or having a friend move away—she might hope that things will be better in the new year. Perhaps she will find a new job or make a new friend. Many people make new year's resolutions to help them become better people. A new year's resolution is a promise you make to yourself, such as: "I resolve—or I promise—to share my toys more with my little brother." Or: "I resolve to do my homework each night before watching television." Or: "I resolve to set the dinner table three times a week." The new year is a good time to make promises to help us become better people.

When God sent Jesus into the world, all people everywhere were given a chance at a new start. Jesus was born to help make people's lives better. Jesus grew up to be a special leader, a leader from God who showed the people of the world just how much God loved them. God's love made people's lives better, and it made them better people.

We still learn about God's love from Jesus today. The love we read about in the Bible is the same love we know from God in our own lives. When we make a mistake, we are forgiven and loved by God, and we don't ever have to make that mistake again. But even if we do make the same mistake, we are forgiven and loved by God again until we get it right. God gives a chance at a new start because God loves us.

Let's Pray. Dear God, thank you for giving us new chances. Each time we make a mistake, help us to learn from it and try harder not to make the same mistake again. In Jesus' name. Amen.

Happy New Year, everybody!

(Either collect the party supplies as the children leave, or let them keep them.)

The St. Luke* Awards

Props Needed

An award such as a trophy, ribbon, medal, certificate, or plaque

A blue ribbon for each child with a loop of masking tape on the back so it can be easily attached to clothing

The Message

I have something really neat to show you this morning. (*Show the prop.*) Can everybody see it? It's a medal. It has a small piece of metal hanging from a ribbon at the top. There's a pin on the back so the person who earned this medal can wear it on his or her jacket. What color is the ribbon? (*Listen to answers.*) It's blue because whoever earned this medal won first place in some kind of a contest. What do you think the winner of this medal had to do to earn it? Did she have to throw a ball the farthest, or play a musical instrument the best, or spell the most words right? What do you think? There is a clue on the medal. If you look very closely, maybe you can figure it out. (*Pause for answers.*) The medal has something to do with music, that's right. How did you know? (*Pause.*) Because there's a picture of a musical note on the front. Very good. This was the first place medal in a contest where people played the piano.

Have any of you ever received a medal or a trophy or a ribbon or a certificate? (*Listen to answers.*) Awards are given for all different kinds of things. People win awards for being good in sports or music, spelling or math. Some people receive good citizenship or service awards for helping others. Our church gives all the children who come to church school a certificate at the beginning of summer for the good work you did in your classes during the fall, winter, and spring. Do you remember getting a certificate last year?

*Your church's name

Earning an award feels really great. You know you did a good job at something, and you feel good about yourself when you look at your trophy or certificate. But the best part of winning an award is when someone who loves you, someone you care about—your teacher, your grandparent, your minister, your mom or dad—puts his or her arm around your shoulder and says, "I'm proud of you."

Just before Jesus started his work of teaching and healing, he went to the Jordan River to be baptized by his cousin, John the Baptist. When John baptized Jesus, he walked out into the river, said a prayer, gently lowered Jesus all the way into the water, and then helped him back up again. Now Jesus was ready to begin the difficult job God had given him to do.

When Jesus was coming out of the water, the Spirit of God came down from heaven. It looked like a dove and landed on Jesus' shoulder. Then God spoke from heaven and said, "You, Jesus, are my son, whom I love very much. I am proud of you." Jesus must have felt pretty good, knowing that he had God's love and support as he began his ministry.

I want each of you to know that God loves you, too. God is proud of you just for being who you are—and so am I. I have a blue ribbon for each one of you to help you remember how special you are. (*Stick a ribbon on each child.*)

Let's Pray. Dear God, thank you for building us up with your love and support. Help us to build each other up as well. Amen.

Who Said That?

Props Needed
Flannel board
Flannel-board figures (found in the Appendix)

The Message
There are many stories about prophets in the Bible—stories about good prophets as well as stories about bad prophets. The good prophets in the Bible were men and women who worked for God by delivering God's messages to the people. Sometimes the people liked the messages they heard, but most of the time they did not like what the prophets had to say. Too often the people had disobeyed God and were being told to shape up or else. Being a prophet who had to deliver bad news was not an easy job, but good prophets did it anyway because they loved God. Today we're going to talk about one of God's first and very best prophets. He lived thousands of years ago, even before Jesus, and his name was Samuel.

When Samuel was a little boy, only two or three years old, his mother brought him to the temple at a place called Shiloh. She left him at Shiloh to live with Eli, the old priest who was in charge of the temple.

We might think it was strange for Samuel's mother to leave her little boy with the priest, but she did it to keep a promise to the Lord. Before Samuel was born, she had promised God that if God gave her a child, she would give the child back to do God's work. So Samuel's mother brought her boy to the temple and left him with Eli. Samuel's parents visited him each year when they went to Shiloh to worship, and they loved their boy very much.

Several years had gone by and one night Samuel was lying down in the temple. (*Set up building outlines on flannel board and follow story with figures.*) Eli was sleeping in his room when Samuel heard someone calling his name. Samuel thought Eli had called him, so he ran to Eli's room and said, "Here I am. You called me." Eli said, "No, I didn't call you. Go back to bed." So Samuel went back to the temple and lay down. Again he heard a voice call, "Samuel!" Again he went to Eli's room and said, "Here I am. You called me." But Eli said, "I did not call, my son. Lie down again."

Who do you think was calling Samuel's name? (*Pause for answers.*) God was, that's right. But Samuel was still young and didn't know much about God yet. So when he heard the voice call his name for the third time, he went into Eli's room again. Finally Eli figured out that God must have been the one calling Samuel's name. So he said to Samuel, "Go back to bed, and if you hear the voice calling you again, say, 'Speak, Lord. I, your servant, am listening.'" Samuel did as he was told. He lay back down in the temple, and when he heard a voice calling "Samuel! Samuel!" he answered: "Speak, Lord. I, your servant, am listening." Then God spoke to Samuel.

From that day on, Samuel served the Lord as a prophet. He brought God's message to the people whether they wanted to hear it or not.

Each of us is called to be God's servant, too. We may not hear God's voice in the night as Samuel did, but the Bible tells us that all who love God should help make this world a better place. Sometimes that means standing up for what's right, even if it's not the popular thing to do, just like Samuel did.

Let's Pray. Dear God, thank you for showing us how to be faithful servants through people like Samuel. May we always answer your call with an eager "Here I am." Amen.

God's Fishing Tips

Prop Needed
A fishing lure

The Message
Have any of you ever gone fishing? (*Pause for answers.*) What things do you need to catch fish? (*Listen to answers.*) Yes, you need a fishing pole and a reel, a net, hooks, line, and bait. There are several different kinds of bait you can use when you want to catch fish. You can use worms, salmon eggs, pretend bugs called flies, or even cheese.

Some people don't use bait to catch fish. They use something called a lure instead. (*Show prop.*) See how colorful and shiny this lure is? It has a hook on the bottom of it, doesn't it? To use a lure, you tie it to the end of the fishing line, then cast, or throw it into the water. The lure turns in the water, and light reflects off it. When fish see this beautiful, sparkly thing, they come to take a closer look. They are attracted to it, they bite at it, and before you know it, you're reeling in a fish.

When Jesus was just beginning his work for God, what we call his ministry on Earth, he met two brothers named Simon and Andrew who were fishermen. Jesus said to Simon and Andrew, "Follow me and I will make you fish for people" (Mark 1:17). Right then and there, they put down their fishing equipment and followed Jesus. Simon and Andrew were Jesus' first disciples.

Now, if you were fishing for people, what kind of bait would you use? Some people might try to attract others with money, fancy clothes, or powerful friends. But Jesus was poor, wore a simple robe, and had friends who were looked down upon by those in power.

What attracted people to Jesus was something all people need very badly, but something that no amount of money or power can buy. Fishing for people, the lure Jesus used was love. Jesus showed God's love in everything he said, everything he did, and all that he was. People saw that love shining from Jesus—that beautiful, irresistible love of God—and were attracted to it. The closer they got to Jesus, the better they understood God and what it means to be God's children.

We are still attracted by God's love. It is what brings all of us together and makes us one family—the family of God.

Let's Pray. Dear God, we are hooked on you, Lord. Thank you for bringing us into community with your love. Amen.

School Days

Props and Preparation Needed

A backpack containing a notebook, a pencil box, a textbook, and a lunchbox. Fill the lunchbox with orange slices, crackers with peanut butter, cookies, or some other treat (optional)

The Message

I brought a backpack with me this morning. Let's see what's inside. (*Unzip backpack.*) What do you see inside the backpack? (*Pause for answers.*) Yes, we have a notebook, a pencil box, a math book, and a lunch box. (*Remove each item as it is mentioned.*) If you had a backpack filled with these things, where would you probably be going? (*Listen to answers.*) You'd probably be going to school, wouldn't you?

How many of you go to school? Do some of you go to preschool or nursery school? Do some of you go to kindergarten or elementary school? What are the names of your schools? (*Listen to answers.*) I know one school all of you attend—church school.

There are at least two things that all schools have in common, two things that make all schools alike, whether you're talking about James Madison Elementary, The Learning Station Preschool, or the church school here at Westminster Presbyterian. All schools have students, and all schools have teachers.

You all have teachers in your schools, don't you? I know we have teachers in our church school classes. Think for a minute about your favorite teacher. What makes that teacher so special? Why is she or he your favorite? (*Pause for answers.*)

When Jesus was thirty years old, he started doing the work that God had sent him to do. Before that Jesus was a carpenter and built things out of wood. But at thirty Jesus was ready to begin God's special work. We call that work ministry.

Part of Jesus' work—or ministry—was to be a teacher. Remember last week when we talked about Jesus choosing twelve people to follow him? Can you remember what those twelve people were called? (*Pause.*) Disciples, that's right. Disciple is another word for student. The disciples called Jesus "rabbi," which means teacher.

So one of the things Jesus did in his ministry was teach. He taught the twelve disciples and other people who would listen about God's love. He taught them about the Reign of God. He taught them about how God wanted them to live, and about how good life can be when we love God and other people unselfishly. Most of all, he taught them that God loved them no matter what and forgave them when they made mistakes.

The people soon understood that Jesus was no ordinary teacher. Jesus loved and cared about his students, and he made learning interesting, like all good teachers do. But the real reason Jesus was an extra-special teacher was that his lessons came from God.

You and I can still learn from Jesus' teachings today. Jesus' lessons about God's love, and all the other important things he taught are written down for us in the Bible. I'm glad that all of you are here so that you can learn with all of us in the church the lessons that Jesus, the great Rabbi, has to teach.

Let's Pray. Dear God, thank you for sending us the greatest teacher. Help us to be good students—good disciples—and live the lessons Jesus has to teach. In Jesus' name we pray. Amen.

(Pass out treats as the children return to their seats.)

Doc and Rev

Prop Needed
A doctor's kit, either toy or authentic

The Message
Have you ever been really sick? When you were really sick, where did your mom or dad take you to help you get well again? (*Pause for answers.*) To the doctor, that's right. When you're sick you go to the doctor, and the doctor gives you a checkup to find out what's wrong. The doctor is like a detective, looking for clues to what is making you sick. The doctor uses different tools, or instruments, to help find the clues.

I have a doctor's kit with me this morning. You'll probably recognize the tools inside from your visits to the doctor. Who know what this is? (*Hold up stethoscope and listen to answers.*) A stethoscope. Why does the doctor use this instrument? (*Pause.*) To listen to your heart and lungs, that's right. (*Repeat this process with three or four other instruments.*)

Once the doctor decides what's making you sick, he or she tells you what to do to get better. Some of the things the doctor might tell you are to rest, drink lots of juice, use nose drops, and take some medicine that mom or dad can get at the drugstore. After you follow the doctor's directions, you begin to feel better, and once your nose stops running and your head stops hurting and your fever's gone, you're all better. Another word for "all better" is healed.

Last week we talked about how teaching was a part of Jesus' work—or ministry. Healing was another important part of the work Jesus did for God. Jesus helped blind people to see and crippled people to walk. Jesus healed people who had terrible skin diseases and people whose sicknesses were in their minds. Jesus healed all different kinds of people with all different kinds of problems—all without a doctor's bag, tools, or medicine.

Jesus' healing ministry made him famous and very popular. Wherever Jesus went, people brought the sick for him to cure.

But Jesus didn't heal people in order to be liked. He did it to show the people how powerful God was and how much God loved them.

Teaching and healing were two big parts of Jesus' ministry. Jesus also spent a lot of time preaching to the people, sharing God's message of love and forgiveness with them. Jesus traveled from town to town with the disciples so that he could preach God's message to as many people as possible.

So teaching, healing, and preaching were the three main duties that Jesus had in the work that God gave him to do, in what we call Jesus' ministry. And all that Jesus did—whether teaching, healing, or preaching—was done with love.

Let's Pray. All-loving God, we thank you for Jesus and his ministry, showing us the way to you. Amen.

Running the Race

Prop Needed
A pair of running shoes

The Message
The last couple of weeks we've been talking about the special work that God gave Jesus to do in the world—Jesus' ministry. Do you remember what the three parts of Jesus' ministry were? (*Listen to answers.*) Jesus' ministry included teaching, healing, and preaching, that's right. And everything that Jesus did was done with love.

All those many years ago, Jesus' disciples helped him with his ministry. Jesus doesn't live here on Earth the same way he used to, and the twelve disciples died and went to heaven a long time ago, too. Who do you think carries on Jesus' ministry today? Who teaches about God, shows the world the power of God's love, and shares the good news of God's love and forgiveness with people who've never heard it or need to hear it again? (*Pause for answers.*) The church does, that's right. All of us who believe in Jesus and love Jesus are the modern-day disciples, and Jesus is counting on us to keep doing the work God gave him to do.

So our church builds schools in places where there are no schools. Our church has schools in places such as Africa, Asia, and Central and South America. In our schools children like you learn how to read and write and do arithmetic. And they also learn about God's love because Christians they've never met cared enough about them to build them a school. Our church is doing Jesus' teaching ministry.

Our church also builds hospitals and free medical clinics in places where people wouldn't be able to see doctors without our help. Some of these places are in other countries far, far away from here. Some of the places are right here in the United States. The doctors and nurses give people medical care whether they have money to pay or not. Our church is doing Jesus' healing ministry.

And our church also builds churches and sends ministers all around the world, so that people everywhere may hear God's message preached and worship together. We are doing Jesus' preaching ministry.

Now, when I say "our church," I don't mean Midvale Presbyterian Church all by itself. I mean all the Presbyterian churches in the country. We all work together to make big projects like schools and hospitals and churches happen. You are a part of this important ministry that our church is doing. Part of the offering that you give each week goes to carry on Jesus' ministry around the world. You also help carry on Jesus' ministry right here in Midvale by caring about the people you meet every day and treating them the way you would like to be treated yourself.

Doing Jesus' ministry is not easy. In fact, sometimes it's really hard work. But doing the ministry makes you feel good. How many of you like to run? Have any of you ever run in a race? (*Show running shoes.*) Some people get very serious about running, and they even buy special shoes like these to run in. Running in a race can be very hard, especially if it's a long race. But if you try your very best, if you give the race your all, it feels really good when you cross the finish line.

Doing Jesus' ministry is like running a race. It's hard work, but when we do our best for God, we feel good inside. With God's help we will continue to run a good race, to do Jesus' ministry well.

Let's Pray. Dear God, thank you for this important ministry which you have given us to do. Help us to do it well, so that all people in every corner of the world will come to know and love you. Amen.

A Friend Indeed

Prop Needed

An object that reminds you of a good friend. Tell the children a story from your own experience that relates the object to an act of friendship (as the following illustration does)

The Message

Good morning, everybody. Do you have a favorite cup you like to drink out of? This coffee mug is one of my favorite cups. (*Show prop.*) It's nice and big, and the handle feels comfortable in my hand. But most of all I love this mug because it reminds me of my friend Julie. Let me tell you why.

One day my mom, my little boy Scott, and I were running errands together. We had just been to the post office, and next we were going to meet some friends for lunch. I put Scott in his carseat, Mom got into the car, and I got into the driver's seat. We all had on our seat belts. I was backing the car out of a parking space when *bam*—I hit something. It was another car.

Well, nobody was hurt, and the two cars weren't badly damaged, but whenever there is an accident, the police have to be called, reports need to be filled out, and it all takes a very long time. I knew our friends would be waiting for us at the restaurant.

My friend Julie happened to drive by. When she saw us, she stopped her car and asked if she could help. Then she drove my mother and Scott to the restaurant while I waited until the police officer said I could leave. I really appreciated her help.

Later that day, back at home, the doorbell rang. At the door was a man from the flower shop holding a beautiful bouquet of flowers. The flowers were in this mug, and the card said, "I hope the rest of your day went better. Love, Julie." Now, wasn't that a thoughtful thing to do? There are some people in the world who are always thinking of others. They try to be helpful whenever they can and are wonderful friends to have.

The Bible tells a story about a man who was paralyzed. That means he couldn't move his legs. This paralyzed man had four wonderful friends. Jesus was visiting the town of Capernaum where the paralyzed man lived. Four friends carried the man on a stretcher to the house where Jesus was staying so that Jesus could heal him and make him walk. But there were so many people at the house that the four friends couldn't get near Jesus. So they carried the man on the stretcher up to the roof. The roof was probably made out of dirt and palm leaves because the Bible says that the friends dug through it, making a hole. Then the four friends lowered the man on the stretcher down into the room where Jesus was. Jesus saw how strong their faith was and told the man, "Stand up, and take your mat and go to your home." And he did!

Those four were very good friends to the paralyzed man. They took him to see Jesus, and they didn't give up. Helping their friend was too important to them to give up. And because they had strong faith and kept trying, their friend was healed. He walked home.

Let's Pray. Dear God, thank you for the gift of friendship. We pray that we're the kind of thoughtful people our friends can count on for help. Amen.

A Girl, a Cat, and a Zebra

Prop Needed
A well-worn stuffed animal

The Message
This morning I want you to think back as far as you can to when you were really small. What kind of chair did you sit in for meals when you were one or two years old? (*Listen to answers.*) What kind of bed did you sleep in? (*Listen*). Do any of you remember having a special blanket or stuffed animal like this one that you used to sleep with every night? (*Show prop.*) If you fell down and hurt yourself, or if you were visiting someplace you'd never been before, just holding your blanket or stuffed animal made you feel better, didn't it? Maybe it still does. Our story today is about a girl named Maya, her stuffed zebra Stripes (*name the animal you brought as a prop*), and a kitten called Mischief.

Maya had slept with Stripes every night for as long as she could remember. The stuffed zebra had been a present from Maya's grandpa on the day she was born, although Maya couldn't remember that far back. Stripes had always been there when Maya needed him. Well, almost always. One night Maya got ready for bed. She put her pajamas on and brushed her teeth. Then she climbed into bed for prayers and a story. Suddenly, she noticed that Stripes was missing. Maya looked under the covers, behind the bed, and on the floor. She looked in the hall and the bathroom, then downstairs in the kitchen and living room. No Stripes. Maya started to get worried. She knew she wouldn't be able to go to sleep without her friend. Then she remembered that she had spilled orange juice on Stripes at breakfast—accidentally, of course. So she looked in the clothes dryer and, sure enough, there he was—clean, soft, and good as new. "Silly zebra," said Maya. "You almost missed storytime!"

On Maya's birthday, her mom gave her a furry, gray kitten. She petted the kitten gently and then tried to pick it up, but the kitten jumped out of her hands and ran down the hall. "You'd better follow her before she gets into any mischief," said Maya's dad. "What a great name!" said Maya. "I think I'll call my kitten Mischief."

Mischief turned out to be the perfect name for that kitten, because she was always getting into trouble. She dug in the houseplants, spilling dirt all over the floor. She played in the piles of sorted socks on the bed, getting them all mixed up again. Maya bought Mischief cat toys and a scratching post, but the kitten liked playing with other things better—drapery cords and knitting yarn. When Maya's mom got angry with Mischief, Maya said, "But Mom, she's only a kitten."

One day Maya went to play at her friend Joey's house. When she got home, she went to her room to hang up a picture Joey had colored for her. There was Mischief, right in the middle of Maya's bed, chewing on Stripe the zebra's tail. Stripes was badly torn, and stuffing was everywhere. Maya cried in a loud voice, "No, Mischief! You bad, bad cat! Look what you've done to Stripes! I hate you!"

Maya's mom came running. When she saw the damage that Mischief had done, she put her arms around Maya. "Oh, Maya, I'm sorry," she said. Big tears rolled down Maya's face, and she said, "I never ever want to see that kitten again!"

Later, when Maya was sitting on the couch watching television, Mischief tried to jump up into her lap. But Maya pushed the kitten back down onto the floor. "Get out of here, you stupid cat," she said. Mischief jumped again, only to be shoved away. "You ruined my special zebra," said Maya. "Now who will I sleep with?"

That night when Maya was in bed waiting to hear a story, she asked her father, "How can I go to sleep without Stripes to hold?" Just then Mischief jumped on the bed. "When I was a boy, my dog slept at the foot of my bed," said Maya's father. "He was awfully good company. I'll bet Mischief would be good company too, if you could forgive her for chewing up Stripes. After all, she didn't mean to hurt you. She was just being a kitten."

Just then Mischief rubbed her head on Maya's arm and purred. "Oh, all right," Maya said. "I forgive you. You can sleep here, and I'll keep you company."

Then Maya's mother came into the room holding something. It was Stripes! She had sewn him back together again. He didn't look quite the same—a little lumpier—but it was definitely Stripes. "Now I have two friends to keep me company," said Maya. And soon Maya, Mischief, and Stripes were all fast asleep.

Let's Pray. Dear God, help us to remember to forgive others, just like you forgive us. Amen.

The Good Old Days?

Props Needed
A comic book, a deck of cards, and a light bulb

The Message
Today I have a comic book, a deck of playing cards, and a light bulb. Can anyone tell me what these three things have in common? (*Pause for answers.*) No? A comic book, a deck of cards, and a light bulb all have something to do with Sundays. Let me tell you why.

Do you remember what we call the ten rules that God gave to Moses? (*Pause.*) The Ten Commandments, that's right. Some of the Ten Commandments are "Do not steal," "Do not lie," "Do not swear," "Worship only the Lord," and "Respect your parents." We still try to follow these rules today, don't we? There's one commandment that many of us forget more often than the others, however. It's the fourth commandment—"Observe the Sabbath day and keep it holy."

The Bible explains that the Sabbath is supposed to be a day of worship and rest. After all, even God only worked six days when creating the world. On the seventh day God rested. Sunday is supposed to be a special day of the week, a day given to God.

People used to be more serious than they are today about making Sunday a holy day. It used to be that stores weren't open on Sunday. And because nothing was open, almost everybody had Sunday off from work. More people went to church on Sunday morning, and sometimes Sunday evening too. In some families, children weren't allowed to read comic books on Sunday. They could read only the Bible. Some people didn't play cards or other games on Sunday. Team sports, like football and baseball, certainly weren't scheduled on Sunday mornings. Some families didn't even do anything that might cause *other* people to work on Sunday, like turn on a light (*hold up light bulb*) or the stove. All the cooking for the Sabbath had to be done the day before. That way the person cooking wouldn't have to work on Sunday, and the people at the electric company wouldn't have to work either.

Rules are important, and so is obeying them. But sometimes we can be so worried about doing exactly what the rule says that we forget why the rule was made in the first place. The Sabbath rule was one that had gotten out of hand during Jesus' time. Jesus was always getting into trouble with the religious leaders for doing things they called work on the Sabbath—things like feeding the disciples and healing the sick. The Pharisees said that helping people on the Sabbath was wrong because it was work. And Jesus said, "Don't be ridiculous."

God made the Sabbath a special day so we wouldn't get so busy that we'd forget about worshipping the Lord. And God also knows how important it is to take a break from our work every so often. Rest keeps us healthy, and after a break we are more eager to go back to our work, whether it is school or a job. I don't think God objects if we read comic books or turn on the lights on Sunday. But I also know that it makes God very happy when we take a special part of each week and spend it here in worship. Coming to church each Sunday helps us to keep the Sabbath holy and obey God's important commandment.

Let's Pray. Dear God, help us to obey this Sabbath commandment in the spirit in which it was given. Amen.

Friendship from the Heart

Props Needed
A handmade heart-shaped valentine card
A heart-shaped valentine candy or sticker for each child (optional)

The Message
I'm sure you'll all recognize what I've brought this morning. (*Show prop and wait for children's responses.*) It's a valentine, that's right, because Valentine's Day is this week. What shape is this valentine? (*Pause.*) Yes, it's in the shape of a heart. Many valentine cards and decorations have hearts on them because Valentine's Day is a day to celebrate love and friendship. We talk about love coming from our hearts, don't we? We say, "I love you from the bottom of my heart." In ancient times, people used to talk about love coming from their kidneys, so a man might have said to his wife, "Darling, I love you from the bottom of my kidneys." That sounds pretty funny to us today, doesn't it?

Of course we know that love doesn't really come from any of our body parts—not our kidneys or our hearts. We know that love comes to us as a gift from God. The love we feel for our families and friends, even the love we have for God was given to us by God in the first place. The Bible says, "We love because God first loved us."

The person for whom Valentine's Day is named, Saint Valentinus, loved God very much. He loved God so much that when the emperor said, "Worship my twelve Roman Gods or die," Valentinus chose death. He could not turn his back on his Christian faith, even if it cost him his life—which it did.

There is a legend about Saint Valentinus that probably didn't happen, but it's a nice story anyway. The legend says that while

Valentinus was in prison waiting to be put to death, the jailer asked him to be his daughter's teacher. The jailer's daughter was named Julia, and she had been born blind. Valentinus said yes, and he taught her history, science, and math. He had to read to her because she couldn't see. He also taught her about God and the Christian faith. Julia asked Valentinus if God could hear people's prayers, and he told her yes. Julia told Valentinus that every night she prayed that she could see. The teacher and student then knelt in prayer together, and while they were on their knees, a blinding light flashed. Julia cried, "Valentinus, I can see!" "Praise be to God!" was his answer.

The legend goes on to say that the night before he was executed, Valentinus wrote a note to Julia. In that note he told her to stay close to God, and he signed it "From your Valentine." The next day, February 14 in the year A.D. 270, Valentinus was put to death.

February 14, Valentine's Day, gives us a chance to do nice things for our family and friends, to let them know we love and care about them. We might give them valentine hugs, valentine kisses, or valentine cards.

God sent the greatest valentine in the world to let each and every one of us know how much God loves and cares for us. That valentine was Jesus.

Let's Pray. Dear God, we thank you for the gift of love, for all those who love us, and for those whom we love. Thank you most of all for sending Jesus into the world to share your love with us. Amen.

(You may want to give the children each a valentine card or heart-shaped sticker as they leave.)

Season of Lent

Thy Will Be Done

FIRST SUNDAY OF LENT   God's Covenant with Noah
Genesis 9:8–17

Signs of the Promise

Props Needed

A prism or crystal
A sheet of white paper
A rainbow-striped piece of ribbon about six inches long (optional)

The Message

Today we're going to start our time together with a science demonstration. We need a piece of plain white paper and a prism. (*Show props.*) As you can see, the prism looks like glass. It's clear like glass, and it would break if you dropped it. But the prism is made out of something called crystal. Crystal is much heavier than glass. Carefully hold this, and see how heavy it is. (*Pass around crystal.*) Crystal can also do something that ordinary glass can't do. When light shines through the crystal, what happens? (*Refract a rainbow onto the piece of paper.*) It makes a rainbow, doesn't it?

Some people hang prisms in their windows, and when the sun shines through, rainbows appear on the floor, walls, and ceiling of the room. How many of you have seen a rainbow in the sky after a rainstorm? Rainbows also carry a message, a message from God.

Do you remember the story from the Bible about Noah and the ark? Many years ago, all the Earth's people were bad. They were greedy and selfish, hateful and mean. They had completely forgotten about God, and God knew that they wouldn't change—except for one man and his family. That man was Noah. Noah trusted and believed in God. So the Lord decided to wipe everybody out (except for Noah) and start all over again.

The Lord told Noah to build an ark, and he did, even though his neighbors teased him and made fun of him. Next God told Noah to collect two of every kind of animal on the Earth—one male and one female. Noah collected the animals and loaded them onto the ark. Noah's neighbors must have thought he was really nuts.

Then it started to rain. It rained and rained for forty days and nights. That's more than a month of solid, pouring rain. The water covered the whole Earth, with Noah, his family, and the animals floating safely in the ark. After forty days, the rain stopped. The water started to do down, and the ark rested on a mountaintop.

When the land dried out, God told Noah to come out of the ark and bring his family and all the animals with him. The first thing Noah did when he got out of the ark was build an altar and worship God. This made God so happy that God decided right then and there to never destroy the land, the animals, and all the people again.

God made an important promise to Noah. We call an important promise like this a covenant. God made a covenant with Noah, his sons, and the animals on the ark to never again destroy the Earth with a flood. And God said there would be a sign—or a reminder—of this covenant in the sky. That reminder is the rainbow. Every time we see a rainbow in the sky, we know that God is remembering the promise never to flood the whole Earth again.

God has made many promises to God's people, and we can read about God's promises in the Bible. For example, God has promised to always love and be with us. One of the most important promises God made was the promise of a messiah, someone who would lead the people away from sin and show them the way to God.

We can trust God to keep all of these promises to us. The Earth has not been destroyed by a flood a second time. We know God's loving presence in the special people God gives to care for us—people like parents, friends, grandparents, teachers, ministers, and neighbors. And God sent Jesus to die for our sins and lead us to God.

Let's Pray. Dear God, thank you for the covenants you have made with your people through the ages. Thank you for keeping your promises. In Jesus' name. Amen.

Before you go, I'd like to give each of you a rainbow bookmark. Put it in your Bible and remember that God keeps promises. (*Pass out ribbons.*)

Getting the Whole Story

Prop Needed
A cross, preferably wooden and rustic looking

The Message
This morning I want to tell you a story that many of you may have heard before. If you know the story of Little Red Riding Hood, raise your hand. Most of you know the story. Well, I'm going to tell it to you anyway because you can never hear a good story too many times.

Once upon a time, there was a little girl called Little Red Riding Hood. Her grandmother was sick in bed, so Little Red Riding Hood was taking a basket of goodies to cheer her up. Her grandmother's house was on the other side of a forest from her own house. Little Red Riding Hood's mother handed the girl the basket of goodies, tied her red hooded cape under her chin, and kissed her good-bye. "Be careful," her mother said, "and watch out for the big bad wolf!" Little Red Riding Hood walked out the door and skipped down the path toward Grandma's house.

Now Red Riding Hood didn't know it, but watching her from behind the trees were the hungry eyes of the big bad wolf. He could smell the delicious goodies in the basket, and Red Riding Hood looked pretty tasty herself. The wolf ran ahead to Grandma's house.

When Red Riding Hood arrived at her grandmother's home, she knocked on the door. "Come in, my dear," said a voice from inside. Red Riding Hood opened the door and found her grandmother sitting up in bed, feeling much better. Red Riding Hood poured two glasses of milk and shared the goodies in the basket with her grandma. At the end of the afternoon, Little Red Riding Hood kissed her grandmother good-bye and got home before supper. The End.

How did you like the story? (*Listen to answers.*) You didn't like it? Well, I left out all that scary stuff about the wolf eating the grandmother and trying to eat Red Riding Hood on purpose. That's the part of the story where the bad things happen. I only wanted to tell the happy parts of the story, but you didn't like it.

Actually, I think you're right. For a story to have a really happy ending, there have to be some tough parts in the middle, don't there? Little Red Riding Hood seeing her grandmother after the woodman rescues her by chopping open the wolf who ate her is much more of a happy ending than just knocking on the door and finding her grandma home.

Jesus' life was a lot like this story. Not everything that happened to him was good, even though he was a very good person. Some of the things that happened at the end of Jesus' life were very bad. Sometimes we don't like to think about these things. We'd rather just remember the happy parts of Jesus' life, like the miracles—healing people and feeding the hungry—and the things Jesus taught his followers. But if we ignore the sad things—Jesus being arrested, beaten, and at last killed on a cross (*show prop*)—if we ignore the sad things that happened to Jesus, then we can't know how happy the end of the story truly is. Jesus rising from the dead is not as important without all the things that happened before that—good and bad.

From now until Easter the church will be learning about this sad part of Jesus' life. This part of the church year is called Lent. During Lent we remember the bad things that happened to Jesus and that Jesus loved us enough to go through those bad things for us, and even die for us.

Let's Pray. Dear God, we thank you for all that Jesus suffered so that we might live. In Jesus' name we pray. Amen.

The Money Game

Props Needed

Several quarters, dimes, nickels, pennies, and one foreign coin
A picture of the temple at Jerusalem

The Message

Have you ever played the money game? I show you a coin, and
you have to tell me what that coin is. If you are right, then you
get to keep the coin. Be sure to raise your hand, and don't shout
out the answers, okay? All right, here's the first coin. (*Hold up a
U.S. coin.*) Who can tell me what it is? (*Play several rounds until
everyone has had a turn, if possible.*) Now for the last coin. (*Hold
up the foreign coin.*) Who can tell me what this is? Does anybody
recognize this coin? It's an Austrian schilling. That was a trick
question, wasn't it? This is a foreign coin. It comes from the country of Austria. You can't spend this coin here in the United
States, and you can't spend U.S. money in Austria. This coin
won't fit into our soda pop machines or video games. If you only
had foreign money, you would have to go to the bank, and there
you could exchange the foreign money for U.S. dollars. If you
travel to another country, then you have to trade your U.S. dollars for the money of the country you're visiting. Austria has
schillings, Mexico has pesos, Germany has deutsche marks, Japan has yen, and Israel has scheckels. Remember what it means
to exchange money when we get to that part of the story today.

We start our story, though, with Passover. Passover is a Jewish
holiday that takes place once a year in the spring. It celebrates
Moses leading the Hebrew people out of slavery in Egypt, and it
is a big festival. In Jesus' day, all the Jews who possibly could
went to celebrate Passover at the temple. Jesus was Jewish and
went to Jerusalem for Passover, too. When Jesus got to the city,
he went straight to the temple. The temple was a beautiful building with an inner courtyard, an outer courtyard, and rows of col-
umns all around it. (*Show pictures of the temple.*) When people

worshipped God in those days, they brought animals to sacrifice on a special stone table called an altar. The animals would be killed and cooked on the altar, and only the priests could eat the meat. People came from all over Israel—and from other countries, too—to worship at the temple during Passover. Some people couldn't bring any animals to sacrifice because they had to travel too far. So there were people in the outer courtyard of the temple selling animals for sacrifices. The people who came to Jerusalem from foreign countries didn't have the right kind of money with them to buy the animals, so there were also money changers in the courtyard. The money changers traded, or exchanged, the money of other countries for Israel's money. Then the foreign visitors could buy the animals they needed for sacrifices.

When Jesus came to the temple to worship and saw all of these people doing business in the courtyard, he didn't like what he saw. He didn't like it because the men selling the animals and changing the money were cheating their customers, many of whom were poor. They charged way too much for the animals, and when they exchanged the money, they didn't give the foreign visitors as much Israeli money as they should have. For these men, the sacred worship of God had become a chance to make a lot of money by cheating others, and this made Jesus very angry.

In fact, Jesus became furious. He made a whip and chased all the cheaters and the animals out to the temple courtyard. He threw the coins of the money changers and turned their tables upside-down. He shouted, "Stop making God's house a marketplace!"

The other people standing around the courtyard were more than a little surprised. They said, "Show us why you have the right to do these things." Jesus answered them, "Destroy this temple, and in three days I will build it up again." The people thought he meant the temple building, which had been under construction for forty-six years and still wasn't finished. But when Jesus said "this temple," he was talking about his body. After Jesus was killed on the cross, God raised him to new life three days later. Then Jesus' disciples remembered what he had said that day at the temple in Jerusalem. Then they understood who Jesus was—the Child of God.

Let's Pray. Dear God, may our worship be the pure acts of praise and thanksgiving that you deserve. In Jesus' name. Amen.

Places to Go, Things to Do

Prop Needed
None

The Message

Do you like going places? I like going some places, and other places I don't. I'd rather stay home than go certain places. You can tell whether I want to go somewhere or not just by listening to the way I talk about it. For example, if I say, "I *get* to go to the beach this summer," do you think I want to go? (*Pause for answers.*) It sounds like I'm looking forward to going, doesn't it? What if I say, "I *have* to go to the garage to get my car fixed." Do I sound happy about that trip? (*Pause for answers.*) How could you tell I want to go to the beach but not to the garage? (*Pause.*) When I talked about my vacation, I used the word get—"I *get* to go." But when I talked about the chore of going to the garage, I used the word have—"I *have* to go." "Get to" and "have to" can be clues to how a person feels about something.

I'm sure you have feelings about the places you go and the things you do. Sometimes you get to; other times you have to. What about going to a friend's birthday party. Do you get to go, or do you have to go? How about going grocery shopping with your mom or dad—get to or have to? There are no right or wrong answers to these questions, by the way. However you feel about the place is the right answer for you. Do you get to go to the park, or do you have to go? How do you feel about going out for pizza? To the library? Shopping for clothes? Do you get to or have to go to school? What about going to school on the day of a field trip to the zoo? How do you feel about coming to church? Do you get to come, or do you have to come?

If some of you said you have to come to church, that's okay. I'm glad you're here, even if you weren't exactly excited about coming.

And if you said you get to come to church—if you look forward to coming here each week—that's great too. I'm glad you're here with us also.

Some people think that church is boring. Some people think that the only thing the preacher talks about at church is how bad everybody is, and how we'd better behave better or else we'll be in big trouble with God.

I think that church is an exciting place to be. I almost always feel like I *get* to come to church. And even on those weeks that I come because I have to, once I'm here I'm glad I came. I know that the people here love and care about me, and we all love and care about each one of you, too. Being in a big room full of love gives me a good feeling. There are parts of the church service I especially like, such as the time I share with you each week and the beautiful music. And I like the church dinners and parties we have. But the most exciting thing about church is something that doesn't happen anywhere else. Each week we come together and share the good news of the gospel. God loved the world so very much that God sent Jesus here to show us that love, and everyone who believes in God will be given everlasting life in heaven. Now that is exciting news! You probably won't hear that message at a grocery store, an amusement park, the beach, a pizza parlor, or school. But every week we come together at church to hear and celebrate the message of God's love for each one of us. I think that's pretty exciting.

Let's Pray. Dear God, thank you for the good news of your love, and for this community in which we share that news. Help us to carry that message out into the world. Amen.

A Clean Slate

Props Needed

A chalkboard, chalk, and an eraser

The Message

Do you ever do anything wrong? Do you always tell the truth about what you've done, or do you sometimes try to cover up? (*Listen to answers.*)

Once there was a boy named Michael. Michael was a good boy—most of the time. But one day Michael asked his mother if she would play a game with him while his little sister Lindsey was taking a nap. His mother was very tired and said no, she wanted to have some quiet time to herself and read a book for half an hour. Maybe they could play a game later, she said. Michael kept bugging his mom and wouldn't leave her alone. Finally she told him to go downstairs and play in the playroom.

This made Michael very angry. He went downstairs like his mother asked him to do. He went into the playroom and started looking around at stuff, thinking all the time about how mean his mom was not to play with him. He found some crayons. He thought, *I'll show her,* and he scribbled all over one wall of the playroom.

Later, after supper, when Michael's mother went downstairs to put away some toys, she saw the wall. She called Michael and asked, "Did you color on this wall?" Michael answered, "No, Lindsey did it." His mother knew that Lindsey had not been downstairs since that morning, and the wall had been clean at naptime. "Are you sure you're telling me the truth?" Michael's mother asked. "Will you get really mad at me?" Michael asked. Then he told her that he was the one who had scribbled on the wall, not his sister.

Michael did a very naughty thing. What did he do that was wrong? (*Write answers on the chalkboard.*) That's right, he scribbled on the wall with crayons. And then he lied about what he had done and tried to blame his sister. Did lying help Michael, or did it get him into more trouble? (*Listen to answers.*) Yes, it's wrong to do something you know you shouldn't, and it's even worse to lie about it.

What if Michael had gotten away with the lie? What if his mother believed him and blamed Lindsey for coloring on the wall? Then would it have been okay to lie? (*Listen to answers.*) I don't think lying, especially to our parents, is ever okay. Even if he hadn't gotten caught, Michael would have known inside that he was the one who had broken a rule and then lied about it. But there's someone else who would know too. God. God knows everything we do, good and bad. We can't hide anything from the Lord, and lying about something never works with God.

You want to know something really great, though? God understands. God wants us to be as good as we can be, but when we mess up and do something wrong, even if we lie about it, God still loves us and forgives us.

What are some of the things you have done wrong? (*Write responses on the chalkboard.*) God sent Jesus into the world to share God's love with us and to die for our sins. What that means is that God's love for us is so strong that when we say we're sorry for something we've done, we are forgiven. (*Erase chalkboard.*) God wipes the slate clean and tells us it's okay, but we should try to do better next time.

When we admit to God that we've done something wrong, and we say we're sorry, that's called confession. God doesn't expect us to be perfect but to try our best and to confess or admit when we make mistakes. God's love makes up for the rest.

Let's Pray. Dear God, we confess that we are not perfect. Sometimes we do things that we know we shouldn't. Forgive us, Lord, and help us to do better. In Jesus' name. Amen.

Mark 11:1–11

Palms and Palms

Props Needed
A palm branch
A palm branch for each child (optional)

The Message
This Sunday is the first day in a week we call Holy Week. Each year during Holy Week we remember the things that happened to Jesus during the last week of his life here on Earth. Most of these things were bad, but the week started off with joy and excitement.

Jesus was very popular with the common people of Israel. This was because they saw or heard about his teachings, healings, and other miracles. He had become sort of a celebrity, like a sports hero. News spread to Jerusalem that Jesus was coming to the city, riding on a donkey. People lined up on the sides of the road so they could see him as he came into town.

If Michael Jordan were coming to your town, people would get pretty excited, don't you think? Fans would probably go to the airport, hoping to see him or maybe even get his autograph. Jesus' entry into Jerusalem was like that.

People stood at the sides of the road waiting for Jesus as if they were waiting for a parade to start. Finally someone shouted, "Here he comes!" People pulled branches off nearby palm trees, branches like this (*show prop*), and waved them in the air like pennants or flags. They shouted "Hosanna! Hurray! Blessed is the one who comes in the name of the Lord!" They laid their coats and palm branches in the road for Jesus' donkey to walk on. They welcomed Jesus into Jerusalem as a hero. But not everyone was pleased.

The religious leaders—people called Pharisees, Sadducees, and high priests—did not like Jesus. They were afraid that Jesus was too popular with the people and that the people would listen to Jesus instead of them. The joyful welcome Jesus received as he came into Jerusalem made these leaders even more worried, so they decided to get rid of Jesus.

On Thursday of that week, the religious leaders put their plan into action. Jesus shared the Passover supper with his disciples, but one—Judas Iscariot—left early. The other eleven disciples went with Jesus to a garden called Gethsemane to pray. While Jesus was praying, Judas came into the garden followed by some soldiers. He kissed Jesus on the cheek to let the soldiers know which man was Jesus, and then the soldiers arrested him.

Jesus was a prisoner, and the soldiers treated him very badly. They beat him and teased him. They put a crown made out of thorny branches on his head. Jesus was put on trial, but the witnesses lied about him and said he wanted to overthrow the government, kill the emperor, and take over the country. The judge, Pilate, knew there was not enough evidence against Jesus to prove he was guilty, but the religious leaders spoke against Jesus to the people and stirred them up. The same people who had welcomed Jesus into the city as a hero on Sunday told Pilate to crucify him on Friday. Pilate was afraid of the crowd, so he said Jesus was guilty as charged and gave the order to have him executed or killed.

The way the Romans executed their prisoners was very cruel. They made a cross out of wood and laid the person down on it. Then they hammered nails through the palms of the person's hands (point to your palms) and through their feet. There was a little shelf for the person to kind of sit on, and the cross was raised into the air. The prisoner was left nailed to the cross with no food or water until he or she died. This is what happened to Jesus.

When we think of palms or Palm Sunday, we need to remember the palms that waved in praise and celebration of Jesus at the beginning of the week. We also need to remember the palms of Jesus' hands, and how he was nailed to the cross toward the end of the week. We remember both kinds of palms because both of them tell an important part of Jesus' story, the story which shows God's amazing love for us.

Let's Pray. Dear God, we thank you for all the pain and suffering Jesus went through for our sake. Thank you for loving us enough to send Jesus to live, and even die, for us. Amen.

(You may want to give palm branches to the children as they return to their seats.)

Season of Easter

Breaking Free

Props Needed

An actual cocoon or pictures showing the life cycle of a butter-fly (or both). Cover the pictures and reveal them one at a time as you discuss each step in the transformation process. (Such photos may be found in an encyclopedia.)

The Message

Spring is a wonderful time of year, don't you think? The weather starts to warm up, and you can play outside after being cooped up indoors during the long, cold winter. When you go out-side, signs of new life are everywhere.

Delicate light green leaves start to grow on the branches of trees that have been bare all winter. Other trees show off by being covered with beautiful flowers. Bulbs that have been resting in the ground for months send up flowers like tulips, daffodils, and crocuses. Animals that have been asleep since Christmastime wake up in the spring—animals such as bears, possums, and in-sects. Birds that have been sunning themselves in the warm south fly north again, and all kinds of animals have babies.

One of the most amazing changes that takes place in the spring happens to the lowly caterpillar. Caterpillars hatch from eggs that are usually laid on the twigs of trees. When a caterpillar hatches, it is hungry. In fact, caterpillars spend most of their lives eating, and most caterpillars like leaves. Sometimes trees actually die because all of their leaves are eaten by caterpillars two or three years in a row, and trees need their leaves to live.

Then one day the caterpillar stops eating and starts to do something very mysterious. Do you know what that is? (*Pause for answers.*) That's right, the caterpillar spins a silken thread, at-taches itself to a twig, and makes a cocoon around itself. This is what a cocoon looks like. (*Show prop*).

Time passes. From the outside of the cocoon, it looks like noth-ing is happening, like the caterpillar is dead. But something really incredible is going on. Time passes until one day, the cocoon wriggles on its stem. Slowly the cocoon rips open, and out comes not a caterpillar—but a beautiful butterfly. All that time when it looked like the caterpillar was dead inside the cocoon, it was changing into a butterfly.

Butterflies can help us remember what we are here to celebrate today. Last week we talked about the sad things that happened at the end of Jesus' life, and how he was finally killed on the cross. After Jesus died, some friends put his body in a tomb, which was a cave where dead people were buried. They put a large stone in front of the cave's opening. Imagine that the tomb is like the caterpillar's cocoon.

Three days later, three women who were Jesus' friends went to the tomb. No one had had the chance to get Jesus' body ready to be buried before the Sabbath, so these women were coming back later to do what needed to be done. They were wondering who would be able to roll away the heavy stone for them. When they got to the cave, though, they were surprised because the stone had already been rolled away.

They went into the tomb and saw a young man wearing a white robe and sitting on one side of the cave. The women were afraid, but the man told them, "Do not be alarmed; you are looking for Jesus of Nazareth, who was crucified. He has been raised; he is not here." The women ran from the tomb, feeling frightened and amazed at the same time.

God has a wonderful plan for every caterpillar—that it should break free of its cocoon and become a butterfly. God had an even more wonderful plan for Jesus—that he should break free from death and the tomb and be raised to new life. God has a wonderful plan for each one of us as well—that we can share in this new life with Jesus. We call the new life God gives resurrection. Resurrection is what Easter and being a Christian are all about.

Let's Pray. Thank you, Lord, for all of your wonderful plans. Thank you for making us Easter people. In the name of our resurrected Lord and Savior, Jesus. Amen.

Show and Tell

Prop Needed

A large map of the United States with the states clearly delineated

The Message

We're going to begin our time together this morning by talking about nicknames. A nickname is something that people call you, but it isn't your real name. You may be given a nickname because of something you've done or because of the way you look. When I was a teenager, my friends called me Stretch, because I was so tall. Now some people call me Rev, a short name for Reverend, because I am a minister. (*Use your own examples.*) Do any of you have nicknames? (*Listen to answers.*)

People have nicknames, and so do the fifty states that make up our country. Each state has a formal name—California, Kansas, or Delaware—but each state also has a nickname that tells something about that state or its people. Let me show you what I mean. (*Display the map so everyone can see. As you discuss each state, point it out on the map.*)

This is a map of our country, the United States of America. We live in Arizona, which is this green state here. Does anybody know Arizona's nickname? (*Pause for answers.*) Arizona is called the Grand Canyon State because the Grand Canyon is in it. Florida is called the Sunshine State because it's sunny there all year long. Georgia is called the Peach State because it's famous for growing delicious peaches, and Kansas is called the Sunflower State because sunflowers grow wild there. Virginia is called the Mother of Presidents because eight of our presidents were born there. Washington is called the Chinook State because native Americans of the Chinook tribe are from Washington. Missouri is nicknamed the Show Me State. This is because people from Missouri have a reputation for being very practical. They won't believe anything unless they see it with their own eyes. If you grew a five-hundred-pound pumpkin in your garden and told someone from Missouri about it, she would probably say, "Show it to me; then maybe I'll believe you."

Our story this morning is about a man from the Bible who had a nickname too. His nickname was Doubting Thomas. Even though he didn't come from Missouri, he only believed amazing things if he saw them with his own eyes.

Thomas was one of Jesus' disciples. The women who visited Jesus' tomb and found it empty ran to tell the news to the disciples, but the disciples didn't know whether to believe the women or not. That night the disciples were hiding together because they were afraid the same people who had crucified Jesus would come after his friends next. But Thomas wasn't with them. While the disciples were sitting around wondering what to do next, Jesus appeared. He stood in the room with the disciples, said "Peace be with you," and showed them the sores on his hands and side. The disciples were overjoyed to see Jesus alive. Now they knew that what the women had told them was true: Jesus was risen!

Jesus spoke with his disciples and told them to stop being afraid and get to work. It was now the job of Jesus' followers to carry on the work of God that Jesus had started. Jesus gave them the power they would need to carry out their mission of teaching, healing, and preaching God's message. Then Jesus left.

When Thomas returned, the other disciples told him what had happened, but he wouldn't believe them. He said, "Unless I see the mark of the nails in his hands, and put my finger in the mark of the nails and my hand in his side, I will not believe."

A week later, the disciples were gathered together again, but this time Thomas was with them. Once more Jesus came and stood in the room with them and said, "Peace be with you." Jesus turned to Thomas and told him to see and feel his wounds and believe. Thomas did believe, saying, "My Lord and my God!" Jesus wasn't angry with Thomas for not believing in the Resurrection right away, for having doubts, but he was disappointed in Thomas. Jesus said, "Have you believed because you have seen me? Blessed are those who have not seen and yet have come to believe."

Who are the people who believe even though they haven't seen Jesus in the same way the disciples did? We are. All of us who believe in Jesus even though we can't see his scars have a special kind of faith that Jesus calls blessed.

Let's Pray. Dear God, we thank you for the gift of faith. And when we have doubts or questions, please be understanding and patient with us. In Jesus' name. Amen.

The Work Goes On

Props Needed
Flannel board
Flannel-board figures (found in the Appendix)

The Message
Last week we talked about the risen Jesus visiting his disciples, who were afraid and hiding. One thing Jesus told them was to get back to work carrying out the ministry that Jesus had started. He also gave them the power they needed to do God's work.

Not long after this visit, Peter and John were going up to the temple to pray. (*Follow story using flannel-board figures.*) A man who could not walk from the time he was born was being carried. Every day he lay at an entrance to the temple called the Beautiful Gate and asked people for money to buy food and the other things he needed to live. When he saw Peter and John about to go into the temple, he asked them for money. Peter looked at him and said, "I don't have any silver or gold coins, but I will give you what I do have. . . . In the name of Jesus Christ of Nazareth, stand up and walk." Peter took the man by the right hand and helped him stand up, and right away the man's feet and ankles were made strong. The man jumped into the air and began to walk. He went into the temple with Peter and John, walking and jumping and praising God all the way. The people in the temple recognized who he was, and they were absolutely amazed by what had happened to him. They all gathered around the man, Peter, and John to find out why he could suddenly walk. Peter spoke to the people.

He said, "Why are you so shocked by what has happened? You act is if John and I healed this man ourselves, by our own power or our own goodness. The God whom you came to worship in this very temple has raised his servant Jesus from the dead. You remember Jesus, don't you?" Peter said, "He's the one you handed over to Pilate to be crucified. God raised him from the dead. We know because we've seen him, and because we have faith in Jesus' name, this man has been made strong.

"Now friends," Peter went on, "I know that you did not realize what you were doing when you sent Jesus to be killed. God knew that Jesus would have to suffer and even die before we, God's people, would really understand how much God loves us. Turn away from your sin, turn back to God, and the Lord will forgive you and welcome you into God's family, now and forever."

There grew to be about five thousand people listening to Peter's sermon, and many of them believed what Peter said. But some of the religious leaders didn't believe in heaven, so they didn't like what the disciples were saying about Jesus' resurrection. They arrested Peter and John and put them in jail until the next day. Next week, we'll find out what happened to them.

Let's Pray. Dear God, thank you for the incredible gift of your love for us in Jesus. Help us to carry out the work you started and share the good news of that love in all we do and say. In Jesus' name. Amen.

Christ the Cornerstone

Props and Preparation Needed

Building blocks. Erect a building or tower using the blocks at the storytelling site. Experiment with the construction to make sure that the whole structure collapses when you remove the cornerstone block

The Message

Good morning. Can any of you tell me what your house or apartment building is made of? Is it made of bricks or wood, stone or logs, or does it have aluminum siding on it? (*Pause for answers.*) Many of the buildings in Jesus' day were made of stone, especially important buildings like the temple.

The cornerstone was the most important stone in the whole building because it held up all the others. If the cornerstone was taken out, like this (*remove the cornerstone*) then the building would become unstable and fall down like the blocks did. (*If your church building has a marked cornerstone, mention it to the children and suggest that they look for it on their way out later.*)

Last week, remember, we left Peter and John in jail. The religious leaders of the temple had arrested Peter and John after they had healed a man who had never been able to walk. They had also been preaching about Jesus' resurrection to the crowd that had gathered around. The next morning the disciples were brought before the official Jewish council, called the Sanhedrin, for questioning. It was also the Sanhedrin that had found Jesus guilty and taken him to Pilate to be crucified. Peter and John were not afraid, though. God's Holy Spirit was with them as they answered the questions. Members of the Sanhedrin asked Jesus' friends, "Who gave you the power to heal this man?"

Peter said to them, "Rulers of the people and elders, let it be known to you and to all the people of Israel that this man is standing before you, perfectly healthy, by the name of Jesus Christ of Nazareth. You had Jesus crucified, but God raised him from the dead. It's like the stones used to build a building. You rejected Jesus, but God made him the most important stone in the building, the cornerstone. Jesus is the most important person in the world because through him miracles can happen. People can be healed, and through Jesus the world is saved."

The Sanhedrin sent Peter and John away while they decided what to do. They didn't like what the disciples said, but they couldn't say that the healing wasn't real either. The crippled man, unable to walk for forty years, was standing straight and tall right in front of them. Too many people knew about it.

Then they called Peter and John back into the room. They said if they would stop talking about Jesus and the resurrection, they would be free to go. But Peter and John said that they couldn't stop talking about it—they had to tell the truth. The Jewish leaders let the disciples go anyway because they were afraid of all the people who knew about the miracle.

Jesus is still the cornerstone of our church today. Oh, I don't mean he's a brick or a rock that holds up this building. But Jesus is the most important person in the church because our sins are forgiven through him.

Let's Pray. Dear God, thank you for your great and powerful love. May we share your love with others as Jesus and the disciples did. Amen.

Planning Ahead

Look at the preparation required for next week's story.

Vital Connections

Props Needed

A branch cut from a vine, preferably a grape vine (but ivy or any other type of vine will do). Cut the branch the day before the sermon, so it has a chance to wilt

A small bunch of grapes for each child

The Message

I cut this branch off a vine to show you, but it doesn't look very good, does it? Look, the leaves are all wilted, and the stem is droopy. I cut it only yesterday. Why do you think it looks so sick? (*Pause for answers.*) Do you think it needs water? Where does a branch like this usually get water? (*Pause.*) From the plant, that's right. The plant's roots drink up water from the soil and carry that water to the vine's branches, which then take the water to the leaves so the whole vine can live. When I cut this branch from its vine, I cut off its water, too. I could put the branch in a vase of water. Then would the branch live? (*Pause for answers.*) It may live for a little while in water, like flowers do after you cut them. But the branch receives more from the vine than a good drink. Those roots also carry minerals, fertilizers, and other good things from the soil that the branch needs to live. So this poor branch isn't going to live very long without being attached to its vine.

Another thing the branch won't be able to do without the vine is grow fruit. Some vines—raspberry, blackberry, or grape—grow beautiful, delicious fruit we can eat. Of course, a branch by itself, without a vine, cannot grow any fruit.

Jesus tells us that he is like a vine and we are like his branches. We need to be connected to the vine to live, be healthy, and grow fruit. Now, none of us grows grapes or raspberries. When Jesus talks about his followers growing fruit, he means doing good deed and sharing God's message with others. Our fruit is our ministry—that special work we do for God. If we are cut off from Jesus, we Christians can do none of the good things in the world that Jesus has given us to do. Jesus gives us the things we need to carry out our ministry as a church, just as the vine provides things that the branches need to grow fruit and live. Jesus is the vine, and we are the branches. Cut off from him, we can do nothing. That is one reason we come to church—to stay closely connected to Jesus by worshipping and studying him.

Let's Pray. Dear God, you have given us important work to do in the world. Thank you for giving us everything we need to carry out our ministry through Jesus our Lord. Amen.

Before you leave, I want to give each of you a treat to help you remember that Jesus is the vine and we are the branches. With Jesus' help we can do amazing things for God in this world, and make it a better place for all of God's children. (*Pass out bunches of grapes.*)

Anna Jarvis's Mother

Props Needed
A Mother's Day card
A carnation for each child

The Message
Who knows what special day this is? (*Pause for answers.*) It's
Mother's Day, that's right. Here is a card that someone might
give his or her mother on this day. (*Show prop.*) Did any of you
give your mom a card or do something else special this morning
to wish her a happy Mother's Day? (*Listen to answers.*) Mother's
Day gives us a special chance to do nice things for our moms—
like give them pretty cards or serve them breakfast in bed—to
show them how much we love and appreciate them.

Mothers have been around for as long as there have been people, of course, and Mother's Day has been a national holiday since
1914. The person who had the idea for Mother's Day was a school-
teacher and the daughter of a Methodist minister. Her name was
Anna Jarvis, and she loved her mother very much. When Anna's
mother died after a long illness in 1905, Miss Jarvis wanted to
find a way to honor her and show how much her mother meant
to her.

Miss Jarvis remembered the Mother's Friendship Day picnics
her mother used to help organize back home in Grafton, West
Virginia. The picnics were held for mothers after the Civil War, so
that bad feelings left over from the war could start to heal. Then
the idea came to her to have a national day to honor all mothers.

Miss Jarvis wrote letter after letter to all kinds of important
people who help to run our country, telling them about her idea
for a national holiday honoring mothers. She wrote to governors,
senators, congress members, ministers—even the president. Finally, in 1914, President Woodrow Wilson made Mother's Day a
national holiday.

Miss Jarvis never intended for Mother's Day to become com-
mercialized. She didn't want people to feel they had to buy their
moms big, expensive presents to show their love. She believed

that simple things were better—a pair of slippers, a handmade drawing, a few extra chores, or a flower to wear to church. Miss Jarvis liked carnations best for Mother's Day because they were her mother's favorite flowers.

Mother's Day comes once a year, but our mothers love and care for us every day, just as we love and appreciate them every day. We want to show our mothers our love more than one day a year, too. Hugs, kisses, and saying "I love you, Mom," mean a lot to a mother. One of the best ways to show your love and respect for your mom is to listen to her and to try to be the best son or daughter you can—every day. When you make mistakes, your mom will understand, even if she does punish you "for your own good." But if you try your best all year to show your mom how much you love her, then the special things you do for her on Mother's Day will mean even more to her.

Let's Pray. Dear God, we give you thanks for the gift of loving parents, and today we especially thank you for mothers. Help them to do a good job—to be nurturing, patient, and caring, and help us to be good daughters and sons. In Jesus' name. Amen.

Before you leave, I have something for each of you to give to your mother today. Wish her a happy Mother's Day. (*Hand out carnations.*)*

*This story is based on Sidney Fields, "The Mother of Mother's Day," *Guideposts,* May 1987, 49. Reprinted with permission from *Guideposts Magazine.* © 1987 by Guideposts Associates, Inc., Carmel, New York 10512.

Watching and Listening

Prop Needed

Two metal cans connected with a string to make a toy telephone

The Message

Have any of you ever made a toy telephone like this one? (*Show prop.*) It's just two cans attached together by a long string. Let's see how it works. Kyle, you take this can and stand over here. Kristen, you take this can and stand over there, as far away as you need to go to make the string tight. Kristen, hold your can up to your ear, and Kyle, hold your can up to your mouth and say something in a regular voice—not shouting and not whispering. Say, "Hi, Kristen," or whatever you want to say. Kristen, could you hear him? Now Kristen, you say something back. Kyle, you put the can to your ear and listen. Could you hear her?

Well, that's the kind of toy telephone children used to play with before toy companies made fancy plastic ones or electronic ones that talk back to you.

How many of you have talked on a real phone before? All of you have? Who are some of the people you call and talk with on the phone? (*Listen to answers.*) What is it called when you talk back and forth with a friend? We're doing it right now. What is this called? (*Pause.*) A conversation, that's right. When you talk back and forth, sharing ideas, telling another person what you're thinking and feeling and listening to what he or she has to say, that's called having a conversation.

We have conversations with other people all the time, don't we? We can also have conversations with God. Do you know what a conversation with God is called? (*Pause.*) That's right, prayer. Prayer is simply having a conversation, or talking, with God.

There are many different kinds of prayers. With prayers of praise and thanksgiving we say how great we think God is and thank God for all the wonderful things we have been given. With prayers of petition we ask God for things. And with intercessory prayers we pray for other people.

Those are fancy names, but prayers of praise and thanksgiving, prayers of petition, and intercessory prayers are all simply talking with—or having a conversation with—God.

One place we pray is in church. But you can pray anywhere at any time. Sometimes it helps us to concentrate if we close our eyes and fold our hands, but you don't have to. You can pray at home, at school, or even when you're playing in the backyard, and no one else has to know about it. You can just think the words in your head—you don't even have to say them out loud—and God will hear you.

God hears and answers our prayers. Sometimes we may not get the answer we want. God sometimes says no. But the Lord will always give us the answer we need.

Sometimes when people wait to hear God's answer to their prayers, they expect God to talk to them like I'm talking to you now. They expect to hear God speak with a voice. Some people *have* heard God's voice. We read about the prophets in the Bible carrying on conversations with God like with their next-door neighbor. But most of the time God doesn't work that way. Sometimes God answers our prayers by changing a situation, like when a sick friend gets better or our lost dog is found. Sometimes God answers our prayers by giving us advice or helping us through another person such as a parent or a teacher. And sometimes God answers our prayers by changing our hearts, by helping us to accept a hard situation such as a grandparent dying or a friend moving away. And sometimes God answers us by helping us to decide what is the right thing to do.

There is a saying, "God works in mysterious ways." We never know when or how God will answer our prayers, but we do know that God answers. It is up to us to watch and listen for the answers that are part of our conversation with God.

Let's Pray. God, we thank you for caring about us enough to listen to our prayers and answer them. Help us to show you the same courtesy and to watch and listen for your answers. In Jesus' name. Amen.

Happy Birthday

Props Needed

A party hat and balloon for each child

A birthday cake with candles (with someone in charge of the cake out of sight, ready to light the candles and enter on cue)

The Message

We're having a birthday party today. Does anybody know whose birthday we're celebrating? (*Pause for answers.*) Today is Pentecost Sunday, when we celebrate the birthday of the church. All churches around the world are celebrating today, because Pentecost is not just the birthday of our own Westminster Presbyterian Church here in Wilkes-Barre, but the birthday of all churches everywhere. Let me tell you why.

The disciples were all together in a house in Jerusalem for the Jewish holiday of Pentecost. In fact, Jewish people from all different countries were in Jerusalem for the holiday. All of a sudden, there was a loud sound coming from heaven, like a rushing wind during a bad storm, and the sound filled the house where the disciples were. Then flames that looked like they were from a fire appeared in the room, and one flame rested on each of the disciples. The flames didn't burn the disciples though. All of the disciples were filled with God's Holy Spirit, and they began speaking in languages that the people visiting Jerusalem from foreign countries could understand.

People all over the city heard the strange sound of the wind and followed it to the house where the disciples were. They heard their own languages being spoken and were amazed. The people said, "How can these ordinary men know all these different languages? Aren't they all from Galilee? They must be drunk from too much wine."

Then Peter stepped forward and told the crowd that the disciples were not drunk. He said that the reason all the different people could understand in their own languages what the disciples were saying was because God had given the disciples the gift of the Holy Spirit. God's Holy Spirit is the power of God at work in each one of Jesus' followers. The Holy Spirit took a group of Jesus' friends and turned them into the church that day. God's Holy Spirit is what gives us the power to be the Church of Christ today as well.

So on Pentecost Sunday we celebrate, along with every other Christian around the world, our birthday as Christ's church. To have a proper party, we need certain things, don't we? We need hats. (*Pass out the hats.*) Everybody put on your hat, okay? And we need balloons. (*Pass out balloons.*) Did everyone get a balloon? Good. And for a proper birthday party, we need one more thing. What is that? (*Pause.*) Right, we need a birthday cake. Let's everybody—grownups too—sing "Happy Birthday, Dear Church" together. (*Assistant enters with the cake candles lit, and everyone sings.*)

The birthday boy or girl usually blows out the candles on the cake, right? Well, we are all the church, all of Jesus' friends, so on the count of three, let's all blow out the candles. Ready? One, two, three! (*Blow.*)

Let's Pray. Dear God, thank you for giving us the gift of your Holy Spirit and making us the church. May we serve you well. Amen.

(*Let the children know when and where they will get to eat the birthday cake.*)

Season after Pentecost

Abracadabra

Props Needed

A magic wand

A magic trick, if possible (props for simple magic tricks, such as the needle through the balloon illusion, may be purchased at magic and joke shops. Libraries also have books of tricks that can be performed with household items. Or perhaps someone in your congregation can perform a trick for the story.)

The Message

How many of you like magic? Then you know what this is, right? (*Show magic wand.*) Right, it's a magic wand. How many of you have seen a magic show—maybe at a birthday party, at a fair, or on television? Right before the magician does the exciting part of the trick, he or she says a special magic word. What was the magic word of the magician you watched, do you remember? (*Pause for answers.*) Did someone say abracadabra? Abracadabra is the magic word used by most magicians.

Well, since you all like magic so much, we have a magic trick to perform for you this morning. (*Bring out any necessary props and/or magician.*) When it's time to say the magic word, all of you help me out by saying abracadabra, okay? Okay, here we go. (*Perform the illusion and have the children say abracadabra at appropriate point.*)

That was a pretty neat trick, wasn't it? I couldn't have done it without your help. Thank you.

Abracadabra is a long, funny word, isn't it? Some people who study words and where they come from believe that abracadabra comes from the initials, or first letters, in three words from the Hebrew language.* Those words are Ab, which means "father,"

---

*Information found in *Benèt's Reader's Encyclopedia,* 3d ed. (New York: Harper & Row, 1987). Sermon application suggested by the Reverend Robert Zanicky.

Ben, which means "son," and Ruach Acadasch, which means "Holy Spirit." Abracadabra—Father, Son, and Holy Spirit. Those are the three ways in which we understand God. Together, God the Father, God the Son, and God the Holy Spirit are called the Trinity.

The Trinity is something that is kind of hard to understand, but if we want to know God, then we need to try and understand the Trinity. We believe God is one personality in three forms. There is the parent God who created and cares for the world. God's Child lived on Earth, died for our sins, and was resurrected again. The Holy Spirit is the part of God that lives in each of our hearts and helps the church carry on God's work today. But they are all one God. That may sound impossible, but it isn't.

Let's use Jenny's mom as an example to help us understand this three-in-one idea. Jenny's mom is a mother, right? Of course—she's Jenny's mom. But Jenny's mom is also a wife. She's married to Jenny's dad, Mr. Smith. And Jenny's mom is also a daughter. She's the daughter of Mr. and Mrs. Morton, Jenny's grandparents. She is a mom, a wife, and a daughter. She does different things for Jenny as a mom than she does for Mr. and Mrs. Morton as a daughter. She washes Jenny's clothes, for example, but she doesn't wash her mom and dad's clothes. She sends her parents Mother's and Father's Day cards, which she doesn't do for Jenny. But even though she is a mom, a wife, and a daughter, she is still one person—Emily Smith. (*If you can, choose for your example a child whose parents and grandparents the children know.*)

Abracadabra. Next time you hear that magic word, remember how special it really is because it reminds us of God—Father, Son, and Holy Spirit.

Let's Pray. All-powerful and everlasting God, help us to learn about and understand you better every day. You put the magic in our lives, Lord, and we are truly grateful. Amen.

Christ's Hole-y Body

Props Needed

Ten paper or Styrofoam cups that you have altered in different ways—tear the top off one, cut a large wedge down the side of another, cut a hole in the side of one cup, completely remove the bottom from another, and so on

Two whole cups

A ball-point pen or Phillips-head screwdriver

A cup of water

The Message

This morning I brought something very ordinary to show you— a plain paper cup. (*Show whole cup.*) There's nothing exciting about it, but a cup like this is very handy when you are thirsty and need a drink. It could also be helpful for washing out your brush when you're using water colors or as a vase for wildflowers. There are actually many uses we could think of for a paper cup. Can you think of any other things for which this paper cup could be used? (*Listen to answers.*) Those are all good ideas.

(*Punch a hole in the bottom of the paper cup using a pen or screwdriver.*) What about now? Would you want to use this cup for a drink of water or a flower vase now? No, you or the table would get wet, right? You might still be able to use this cup to keep your rocks or seashells in, but it would not do a good job of holding anything liquid such as water or apple juice. It isn't a perfect cup anymore.

This cup reminds me of myself. I do certain things well—I read well, I can help people find answers to their problems, and I'm told I throw a good party, but I am not perfect. Are any of your perfect? People aren't perfect, are they? We all make mistakes. All of us are good at some things but could do better at other things. There is only one perfect person who has ever lived, and that is Jesus.

I have some other cups here. They aren't perfect either. (*Show cups and what's wrong with each one.*) None of these cups would hold water very well, would they? What would you do if you were thirsty and these were the only cups you had? (*Listen to answers.*) I have an idea. (*Stack cups inside each other, lining up the imperfections so that they compensate for each other and the stack as a whole will hold water.*) Now watch this. (*Pour water into the stacked cups.*) What do you think of that? By themselves, none of these cups were any good for getting a drink, but together they can hold water.

The church is a lot like these cups. Just one person alone would not be able to do all of God's work. There's too much that needs to be done for one person to have the time, energy, or talent to do everything. That's why God put us in the community called the church, because when we all work together, we can do great and wonderful things for God. Together we can do much more than any one of us could ever do alone. And Jesus, the world's only perfect person, is the head, or the leader, of the church. (*Put a whole cup on the top of the stack, being careful not to spill any water sitting in the top of the cup.*)

Let's Pray. Dear God, we thank you for giving us this special community called the church to which we belong. May we continue to work together for your glory. In Jesus' name. Amen.

The "In" Crowd

Props Needed

Pictures of young people dressed in popular garb of the 1960s. Photographs, pictures from a magazine or book, a yearbook from the 1960s, or the drawing found in the Appendix may be used

The Message

I have some pictures I want to show you this morning. (*Show the pictures, pointing out some of the fashion details that may seem the most funny to the children.*)

So what do you think? Would you want to wear bell-bottomed pants, or shirts with big, wild flowers all over them, or headbands, or love beads? How do you think the people in the pictures look? (*Listen to answers.*) You think they look funny?

These are pictures taken of people in the 1960s. Most teenagers in the 1960s dressed like this. Your parents may have worn bell-bottomed pants and long hair when they were fifteen or sixteen years old.

Why do you think kids dressed so funny back then? (*Pause for answers.*) Because everybody else did, that's right. They didn't think they looked funny. They thought they looked really cool. They wore bell-bottomed pants, mini skirts, headbands, and love beads so that they would fit in, so that they could be like their friends.

In the 1920s, when your great-grandparents were probably young, kids used to swallow live goldfish. Why? Because everybody else was doing it. In the 1950s, when some of your grandparents were teenagers, the "in" thing to do was to get all your friends together and see how many of you could squeeze into a phone booth.

People like to feel that they belong. Everyone likes to have friends, and no one wants to feel like an outsider. And people have always done some pretty crazy things just because everyone else was doing them, to be a part of the crowd. I'm sure that when your children look at some of the clothes we wear today or listen to the music that is popular now, they'll think we were pretty weird. Some of the things we want to do to be a part of the crowd are fine. Things like wearing bell-bottomed pants and stuffing ourselves into phone booths won't hurt us. But sometimes we might want to be a part of the crowd so much that we think about doing things that can hurt us. Things like disobeying our parents, smoking, using drugs or drinking alcohol, skipping school, stealing from a store, or taking stupid dares—like walking across a railroad trestle or diving into a pond that may not be deep enough—all of these things can really hurt us and are not worth doing just so that other people will like us better.

Remember, if you like yourself, then other people will like you too. If you do things that you know are wrong, you're not going to like yourself very much. And people who ask you to do things that are wrong are not your friends. Friends don't want their friends to get hurt. Friends care about each other and help take care of each other.

If you ever have questions about what is the right or wrong choice to make, talk about it with a grownup you trust. Your mom or dad, a teacher, or I would be glad to listen and help. And you can always talk to God in prayer—about anything. God will listen and guide you to the right decision and to friends you can trust.

Let's Pray. Dear God, there are many choices for all of us to make as we grow up. Help us, your children, make healthy choices. Amen.

Powerful Seeds

Props Needed
A large, clear-glass pitcher of water
A bottle of red food coloring
A medicine dropper

The Message
We're going to start our time together this morning with a science experiment. I have a pitcher of water. (*Show pitcher.*) I want to make this clear water red, so I also have some red food coloring and a medicine dropper. Let's fill the medicine dropper with the food coloring. Lori, will you please carefully squeeze one drop of the red color into the water? We don't want to use too much, because we don't want the water to be dark red, just a nice, bright color. (*Have a child add one drop to the water.*) What happened? Is the water red? Does it look any different? (*Listen to answers.*)

Maybe we need another drop of food coloring. Jim, would you please put one drop in for us? (*Have the children continue adding food coloring, one drop at a time, until the color begins to change.*) Do you notice anything? The water is finally turning red, isn't it? All those drops before, and nothing happened. Now, all of a sudden, the water is changing color. Let's try a few more drops and see what happens. Ah, now it is red at last.

Wasn't that strange? We put in drop after drop of red food coloring, and the water stayed clear. Then, within just a few drops, it changed from clear to pink to red. The first drop didn't seem to do anything, but what would have happened if we hadn't put in that first drop of red? We'd still have a pitcher of perfectly clear water, wouldn't we? All of the drops working together, even the first ones that didn't seem to do anything, are what made the water red. And it all started with one drop.

The Reign of God is like that. When the church started, it was very small, like one lonely drop of red in a huge pitcher of clear water. But slowly, the church started to grow. More people heard the message of God's love and believed the story the disciples told about Jesus' death and resurrection. The church grew bigger and bigger, and today there are millions of Christians around the globe, all trying to make the world a better place. And it all started with a few people who followed a teacher named Jesus.

Sometimes we look at the problems of the world, and they look so big that we don't think we can possibly solve them. We think of things like world hunger or world peace and wonder what we could possibly do to make a difference. But with God all things are possible, and the answers to all problems have to start somewhere. That can of food you bring to the food pantry and that friend that you make up with after a fight—these are important steps toward finding the answers to the world's problems. Each little step is a drop that, when added to all the other drops contributed by the millions of other Christians in the world, will make a difference and make our planet a better place to live.

Let's Pray. Dear God, thank you for the small things that, when added together, make a big difference. In Jesus' name. Amen.

The Mighty Fall

Props Needed
Flannel board
Flannel-board figures (found in the Appendix)

The Message
Are you ever told that you're too young to do something you'd really like to do? Do you ever wish you were a grownup already so you wouldn't be told you're too young anymore? What kinds of things do you wish you could do that you aren't old enough or big enough to do yet? (*Listen to answers.*) Our story this morning comes from the Old Testament in the Bible. The Old Testament is a collection of stories about things that happened before Jesus was born. This story is about a young boy everyone thought was too small and too young and how he surprised them all. (*Follow story using flannel-board figures.*)

The boy worked as a shepherd for his father, and he was the youngest in a family with eight sons. His three oldest brothers were soldiers in the army of Israel, under the command of King Saul.

One day the boy's father asked him to take some food to his three brothers at the battlefield, where they were getting ready to fight the Philistines. When the boy arrived, the two armies were lined up, ready to fight. As the boy talked to his brothers, a huge soldier came forward out of the enemy's army and challenged anyone in Israel to fight him.

When the Israelites saw the huge man, covered in heavy armor and carrying an enormous spear, they all ran. They were afraid to fight him. The shepherd boy asked the soldiers around him why they were afraid. "Who is this Philistine that he should challenge the armies of the living God?" he asked.

When the boy's oldest brother, Eliab, heard him talking with the others, Eliab became angry. "What are you doing here anyway?" he asked. "You have just come down to see the battle."

The king heard about the brave boy and sent for him. The boy offered to fight the huge Philistine, but the king said, "You can't fight him. You're just a boy." But then the boy told the king how he had killed bears and lions to protect his father's sheep. He argued that God, who had saved him from the paws of the lion and the bear, would also save him from the hand of the Philistine. So the king agreed to the fight.

King Saul dressed the small boy in his own big, heavy helmet and armor and gave him his sword, but none of the stuff fit, so the boy left it all behind. He took with him only five smooth stones and a slingshot to fight the Philistine.

The boy went out to meet the Philistine. The enemy saw how small and young the boy was and teased him. The boy spoke back, "You come to fight me with a sword and a spear, but I come with the Lord of hosts, the God of Israel."

The Philistine stepped forward in his clumsy armor. The boy rushed toward him, reached into his pouch, and grabbed one of the stones. He put the stone on his slingshot, swung it around a few times, and let the stone fly. The stone hit the enemy right in the middle of his forehead. The huge man fell forward with a loud crash. And that's how the boy, David, killed the mighty Goliath.

Let's Pray. Dear God, we may be small, but with your help we can do mighty things. Show us the good things you would have us to do. Amen.

On Having Enough

Props and Preparation Needed

One plastic sandwich bag of small chocolate candies or peanuts in the shell for each child. Put an obviously varying number of candies in each bag—one or two bags with a whole handful of candy in them, several with just a piece or two, and the rest with amounts somewhere in between

A large bowl

The Message

Good morning, boys and girls. I have a special treat for each of you today, something I think you'll like. (*Pass out the bags.*) Did everyone get a bag? Hold up your bags so I can see that everybody got one. (*Pause.*) Good. Everybody has a bag. But wait a minute. How did that happen? Do you notice anything strange about these bags? (*Pause for answers.*) They aren't even, are they? Joey, your bag is loaded, but look at Jenny's bag. It only has two pieces in it.

Jenny, how do you feel about only getting two pieces in your bag when Joey got so much? (*Listen to answer.*) Did you do anything wrong, so that you're being punished with such a puny amount? Do you think it's fair that you should only get two pieces and Joey gets much more? Joey, do you think it's fair that you should get so much when Jenny gets so little? Does anyone have any ideas on how we could make this gift fair for everyone? (*Listen to answers.*) We could share, couldn't we?

Everyone empty your bags into this bowl. (*Wait.*) Take turns, and each person take a handful and put it in your bag. (*Wait.*) Now everyone should have a fair share. Nobody's bag is stuffed like Joey's bag was before, but he had more than he needed. If he'd eaten all that at once, he'd probably get a stomachache. And nobody got stuck with only one or two pieces, either. Each of us has enough, and nobody has too much or too little. Do you all feel this is fair?

God wants everybody in the world to have enough of what they need to live—things like food, clothing, clean water, heat in the winter, medicine, and a home. But there are people in the world who do not get enough of these things. It's not their fault. They haven't done anything wrong to deserve to be hungry or cold, just like Jenny didn't do anything wrong to deserve to get the smallest amount in her bag. It's the way things are, but that's not the way God wants things to be. God wants all people to be well-fed, healthy, and strong.

We can help make the world more fair by sharing what we have with others. One of the things our church does with the offering we take each Sunday is to help those in need. Sharing is one of the very best ways we can show God our love. Sometimes we talk about the Reign of God. When the world is finally fair, and all people have enough of what they need—including love—then the world will be as God wants it to be. That is the Reign of God.

Let's Pray. Dear God, teach us to share so the world will be fair and no one will be in need. In Jesus' name. Amen.

Planning Ahead

Read ahead to see what assistance you will need next week.

The Obnoxious Guest

Props and Preparation Needed

This story is a dialogue between the storyteller and a hand puppet, so you will need an assistant to work the puppet and be its voice. Set up a small puppet stage in your usual storytelling area (or some other prop behind which the puppeteer can work)

Two pictures colored from a coloring book

The Message

Hi, everybody. I'm very excited this morning because I brought a friend to church with me, and I want you to meet him. His name is Jack. Jack, where'd you go? Come out and meet the children! Jack Rabbit, where are you?

Puppet (P):   Here I am. Sorry I'm late.

Storyteller (ST):   Jack, these are my friends. Everybody, this is Jack Rabbit.

P: Hi, everybody! I'm glad you have a chance to meet me today. I'm sorry I was late.

ST: Yeah, why were you late, Jack?

P: I was finishing up my masterpiece. I wanted to bring it with me to show everybody. Would you like to see it?

ST: Sure, we'd love to. Wouldn't we, boys and girls? (*Pause.*)

P: Okay, I'll be right back. (*Puppet disappears, then comes back holding one of the coloring-book pictures.*) Tah-dah! Isn't that the most bee-utiful picture you've ever seen in your life? I think it should be hanging in a museum. Maybe I could sell my picture for a lot of money, it's so pretty. It's much better than any that Picasso guy painted, don't you think?

ST: It's very nice, Jack. It reminds me of a picture I colored last week. Do you want to see it? I like my picture too.

P: Oh, I guess so.

ST: (*Show picture.*) What do you think?

P: Oh, mine is much better. See how well I stayed inside the lines? And I used many more colors in my picture than you did in yours. No, my picture is definitely the best. I tell you, it should be hanging in a museum.

ST: Jack, I'm glad you like your artwork so well, but I think you're being a little rude about it.

P: What do you mean? My picture is great!

ST: Your picture is nice, Jack, but I have to tell you that when you say your picture is much better than mine, it hurts my feelings. You can like your own picture without bragging about it so much and without being mean to me about my picture. How would you feel if I told you my picture was best?

P: Gee, I wouldn't like that very much.

ST: Of course you wouldn't. It's great to be proud of yourself when you do something well. But it's wrong to put somebody else down, even if that person didn't do quite as good a job as you think you did. You can find good things to say about what the other person did, too, and then you'll both feel good.

P: I'm sorry. I didn't mean to hurt your feelings. Let me see your picture again.

ST: (*Hold up picture.*)

P: Oh, I really like the red apples that you colored on the tree.

ST: Thank you, Jack. It's nice of you to say so. And you're right, you did stay inside the lines very nicely. The children and I always end our time together with a prayer. Would you like to pray for us, Jack?

P: Why sure! I'm the best pray-er in the world. God listens to me better than anybody else.

ST: Jack . . .

P: Sorry.

Let's Pray. Dear God, when we do something well, help us to feel good about ourselves without being obnoxious about it. In Jesus' name. Amen.

Be Careful What You Wish For

Prop Needed
 A toy catalog

The Message
 Do you ever get catalogs in the mail? When we think about going shopping, we usually think about driving to a store, walking in, looking around, deciding what we want, paying the clerk, and then driving home again. But with catalogs, you can shop without leaving home. I get catalogs for clothes, bird feeders, meat, candy, flowers, furniture, camping gear, jewelry, and toys.
 Some people don't like to shop using catalogs; they'd rather go to a store. But even if you don't buy anything from them, it's fun to look through catalogs and dream about what you would buy if you could.
 Here's a catalog I received in the mail. It happens to be a toy catalog. (*Show prop and leaf through the pages slowly.*) Look at all that fun stuff. If you could have anything you wanted on these pages, anything at all, what would you choose? (*Listen to answers.*) Well, believe it or not, getting exactly what we want is not always good, because we may not want the right thing. Our story this morning is about a girl who got exactly what she asked for, even though what she wanted was gruesome.
 Jesus had a cousin named John, and it was John who told people to get ready for God's special leader to come. John baptized many people, including Jesus, in the Jordan River. King Herod was the Jewish ruler at the time that Jesus and John lived, and he was a very bad king. He was the one who wanted to kill Jesus when Jesus was a baby because he was afraid Jesus would take his place as king.
 John the Baptist had made Herod and his wife Herodius angry by telling them that something they were doing was very wrong,

so Herod threw John in prison. Herodius wanted him killed, but Herod knew that John was a man of God, so he was afraid to kill him.

On Herod's birthday, he threw a big party and invited all the important people in Jerusalem. The king's daughter danced at the party to entertain the guests and honor her father's birthday. Everyone liked her dancing performance so much that Herod told the girl, "Whatever you ask me, I will give you, even half my kingdom."

This was quite a strong promise, and all of the guests heard it. The girl asked her mother, Herodius, "What should I ask for?" Now you might think that Herodius would suggest an expensive piece of jewelry, some land, or a new house all for herself, but do you know what Herodius told her daughter to ask for? The head of John the Baptist on a platter. And so the girl did.

When Herod heard what his daughter wanted, he was very sad. But he had promised her anything, and everyone at the party had heard him. So Herod sent his soldiers to the prison right away. They killed John the Baptist and brought his head back to the girl on a platter. She gave it to her mother. I'll bet she wished she'd asked for a necklace, don't you?

When John's friends heard the news, they were very sad, too. They got his body from the prison guards and buried it in a tomb.

Let's Pray. Dear God, not all the stories in the Bible are happy ones. But we thank you that the main point of the book is happy—everlasting life for all your children. We look forward someday to meeting in heaven John and all the believers who went before us. Amen.

God's House

Props Needed

Pictures of churches clipped from magazines, or pictures of churches around your town

The Message

A few weeks ago, we talked about a small shepherd boy who killed the mightiest solder in the Philistine army with a single stone from his slingshot. Do you remember what that boy's name was? (*Pause for answers.*) That's right—David.

David was a young boy when he killed Goliath, but he was brave and had a strong faith in God. And David grew in bravery and faith as he grew in age and size. When he was a man, God chose him to be the King of Israel. God's people were blessed to have David for their king. He turned out to be the best king God's people ever had.

There were many wars in those days, and David led his army to victory over and over again. Israel won almost every battle with David as commander-in-chief, or leader of the army.

When David first became king, the people of God were divided into two countries—Judah and Israel. David reunited God's people. He brought them together again into one nation with one king, which was not an easy thing to do.

David was a musician. He played a stringed instrument called a lyre, and he liked to sing. David wrote a lot of songs, which are grouped together in a book of the Bible called Psalms. Psalms is the hymnbook of the Bible, and David is given credit for writing it.

David was a good king who tried his best to serve his people and to serve God. He loved God with all his heart, soul, and mind, and he did what God told him to do as he led his people. Israel became a rich and powerful nation under King David. And David gave the credit to the Lord, thanking God for all of Israel's success.

David wanted to show God how much he appreciated all that the Lord had done for him and his country, so he decided to build God a house.

I have some pictures to show you. (*Show props.*) Can you tell me what these are pictures of? (*Pause for answers.*) Churches, that's right. Sometimes we call a church a house of God. That's because when God's people come together to worship, God is there with them.

We believe that God is a spirit who can be anywhere and everywhere at the same time. So even though our church, and the Methodist church, and the Baptist church all have their worship services at the same time, God's spirit can be with the people in all those churches at once.

The people of Israel during David's time didn't think like we do. They believed that God could only be at one place at one time. They believed that God lived in a box—the box in which the stone tablets with the Ten Commandments written on them were kept. It was a very fancy box called the ark of the covenant, and the ark of the covenant was kept in a tent. It traveled with the army when there was a war and stayed in Jerusalem the rest of the time.

David felt bad that he lived in a beautiful palace and God lived in a box in a tent. So he told the prophet Nathan that he'd like to build a house—a temple—where God could live and be worshipped in style.

At first Nathan thought building God a house was a fine idea, but then he heard from the Lord. God didn't want to be stuck in a house. God liked living in a tent that could be moved to where the people were who needed help.

Later a temple was built for the Lord. And today there are many, many churches and synagogues. But we know that God is everywhere, not just in the houses we build for worship. We can worship God in this sanctuary, or in a forest, or in our living rooms, or at the beach. We can worship God anywhere, because wherever God's people are, the Lord is with them.

Let's Pray. Dear God, we thank you for always being with us. In Jesus' name. Amen.

TENTH SUNDAY AFTER PENTECOST   Proper 12
2 Samuel 11:1–15   David and Bathsheba

Dangerous Impulses

Prop Needed
None

The Message
Have you ever really wanted something that you couldn't have?
Maybe the thing you wanted was too expensive, or your parents
said you didn't need it, or it belonged to someone else. What is
something you can think of that you really wanted but couldn't
have? (*Listen to answers.*)

I once knew a little girl who, every time she didn't get what she
wanted, would stomp her feet and scream and behave horribly.
Do you know any children who act that way when they don't get
what they want? What are some other ways people act? (*Listen to
answers.*) Some people see something they want and just take it.
What do we call taking something that doesn't belong to you?
(*Pause.*) Stealing or robbing, that's right. And we know that stealing is very wrong, don't we? We can't always have everything we
want. Part of growing up is learning how to accept not getting everything we want without throwing tantrums and without taking
things that don't belong to us.

Grownups sometimes have trouble accepting this lesson too.
King David is one example of a grownup who still had some growing up to do when it came to not getting everything he wanted.
You might think that David had everything he could wish for. He
was king of Israel, he lived in a beautiful palace, he was rich, and
he had God on his side. In those days, men could have more than
one wife, and David had many wives. And he had many servants
too. David lived a busy, happy life.

One day when David was walking on the flat roof of the palace,
he looked out over the city and saw a beautiful woman taking a
bath in her back yard. David decided that he wanted this woman,
whose name was Bathsheba, to be one of his wives.

There was just one problem. Bathsheba was already married—
to a soldier named Uriah in King David's army. But David didn't

let this stop him. He thought, *I am the king. No one can keep me from getting what I want.*

So David arranged with the commander of his army for Uriah to have a little "accident." The army was attacking an enemy city, and David told the commander to put Uriah in the very front of the fighting. Then, when the commander gave a signal, all the other soldiers were to take two or three giant steps backward, leaving Uriah out in front all by himself. Of course, Uriah was killed. A messenger was sent to Jerusalem to tell David that Uriah was dead. David then married Bathsheba, Uriah's wife, and they had a baby boy.

Do you think what David did was right? Just because he was king, was it okay for him to have a man killed and then steal his wife? (*Pause.*) Well, God didn't like David's behavior, either. David was thinking so hard about what he wanted that he didn't stop to think for a minute about whether what he was doing was right or wrong. When the prophet Nathan told David how angry and disappointed God was, David felt ashamed and sorry. But it was too late. Uriah was dead, and David's feeling guilty would not bring him back to life. God punished David for his sin, but God still loved David and stayed with him as he ruled his people.

I told you last week that David was the best king Israel ever had, and he was. Even the best person makes mistakes. It helps sometimes if we think things through before we act—try to imagine how our actions will affect other people and whether what we do will please God or not. When we do make mistakes, God has promised to forgive us and give us another chance.

Let's Pray. Dear God, we all make mistakes at times. Help us to think through our actions so that our mistakes will be fewer and less hurtful to ourselves and others. In Jesus' name. Amen.

Jamie's Answers

Props and Preparation Needed

Enlarge the story pictures found in the Appendix. Color and mount them individually on pieces of construction paper or file folders. Stack the pictures in order, face down, on your lap. Show them as you tell the story

The Message

Do you ever become very angry when you're playing with a friend? Maybe your friend snatches a toy away from you or won't play the game you want to play. What do you do? (*Listen to answers.*)

Do you ever get really, really excited—so excited that you feel all filled up inside? Maybe it's your birthday, or your grandmother is coming to visit. What do you do? (*Pause.*)

All of us have strong feelings sometimes. Part of growing up is learning what to do with those feelings in ways that won't hurt ourselves or other people. Jamie, the child in our story today, has some good ideas. (*Hold up pictures as they correspond to the following numbered descriptions.*)

1. Hi. My name is Jamie. This is my ordinary face, but I have other faces too.
2. This is my angry face. Sometimes I feel so angry I want to hit something.
3. So I hit my pillow, or kick a ball, or play an angry song on my xylophone.
4. This is my excited face. Sometimes I feel so excited I want to bounce.
5. So I turn cartwheels across the lawn, or skip, or spin around in circles.
6. This is my sad face. Sometimes I feel so sad I want to hurt myself.
7. So I cry, or squeeze my stuffed lion, or sit on my mom's lap.
8. This is my happy face. Sometimes I feel so happy I want to sing,

9. or dance, or laugh out loud, or give someone a great big hug.
10. This is my frightened face. Sometimes I feel so frightened I want to hide.
11. So I scrunch down under the covers, or tell someone special I'm scared, or color a picture about being afraid.
12. Daddy says he loves me all the time—when I'm angry, or excited, or sad, or frightened—
13. and that makes me very happy.

Let's Pray. Dear God, we thank you for the gift of our feelings. Teach us how to use our feelings in good ways. In Jesus' name. Amen.

Copy Catters

Prop Needed
None

The Message
We're going to start this morning with a game. Does everyone know how to play "Simon Says"? I'll be Simon, and every time I say Simon says to do something, you do it. If I say, "Simon says stand up," everybody stand up. But if I tell you to do something without saying "Simon says" first, don't do it. If you do, you'll be out of the game. The last person left after everyone else has gone out will be the winner. Ready to play? Okay, Simon says stand up. (*Play the game, doing all the things you tell the children to do, so that they are imitating your actions.*)

Good game, everybody. (*Sit down at storytelling spot again.*) Every time I said Simon said to do something—like stand up—you copied me like you were supposed to. But there were times when I did something without saying "Simon says," and you copied me anyway—everyone except Brian, and that's why he's our winner. "Simon Says" is a fun game.

Today I want to talk about copying what other people do. Another word for copying is imitating. When I stood up and then you stood up, you were imitating me. We imitate each other all the time, sometimes without even knowing we're doing it.

Once there was a mother who used the word *actually* a lot. When her son was only two-and-a-half years old, he started many of his sentences with the word *actually*. "Actually, Mom, Bert has the yellow head." "Actually, Mommy, I'd like peanut butter and jelly." He wasn't copying or imitating her on purpose, but he'd heard her say "actually" all his life, so he just used this big word without thinking about it.

You probably imitate your parents or an older brother or sister without thinking about it. The way you laugh, the way you hold a fork, some expressions you use, or the way you behave when you're angry or sad or happy—any of these things might be imitations of the people in your family because you are with them so much. When you spend a lot of time with someone, a part of that person rubs off on you.

Other times we imitate people on purpose. If you're in a dance class, you imitate the teacher's steps as closely as you can. We want to be like the people we look up to and admire. Maybe you'd like to be smart like your teacher or adventurous like an astronaut. Maybe you'd like to sing like your favorite singer or run as fast as a track star. Maybe you'd like to be kind like your best friend or strong like a superhero. Is there anyone you'd really like to be like? Do any of you have a hero you might try to imitate in some way? (*Pause for answers.*)

Finding the good in people and trying to imitate the things you admire is fine, but you have to remember one thing: no person is perfect. Everybody makes mistakes. Even Superman is made weak by kryptonite. When we copy the good things in other people, we don't want to imitate their mistakes, too.

There is someone we can imitate without worrying about copying mistakes. That someone is God. God is perfect and never makes mistakes. If we try our best to be like God, then we can't go wrong. Copy God's love, kindness, and caring about others. Forgive other people the way God forgives you. Be honest and generous, and don't say mean things against other people. The Bible says, "Be imitators of God, as beloved children, and live in love, as Christ loved us."

Let's Pray. Dear God, thank you for your loving kindness toward all your children. Help us to be more like you each and every day. In Jesus' name. Amen.

THIRTEENTH SUNDAY AFTER   Proper 15
PENTECOST   Communion
John 6:51–58

By Special Appointment

Props Needed

Your datebook or calendar with appointments written in it

Set up on the communion table: a communion plate and chalice, a loaf of bread, juice or wine in the chalice, and a tray of empty communion cups

The Message

(*Pull out your datebook and look at the page for the coming week.*) Boy, I sure have a busy week coming up. Just look at this mess. (*Show the children your datebook.*) This is my datebook or calendar. I write down all the stuff I have to do during the week in this book so I won't forget anything. Look—tomorrow at ten in the morning, I have an appointment to get my car fixed. In the evening, I have a committee meeting at church. On Tuesday afternoon, I have a dentist appointment. On Thursday, I'm meeting a friend for lunch, and at night I'm going to the play at the high school. (*Use examples from your own schedule, and use the word "appointment" often.*) I get tired just thinking about all those appointments.

Do you all know what an appointment is? An appointment is when you make plans ahead of time to meet with another person for a particular reason. You might make an appointment with your doctor for a checkup. You might make an appointment with your teacher to stay after school for extra help. Or you might make an appointment with a friend to play together on the weekend.

I'd like you to follow me over to the communion table, because I want to tell you about a special appointment we have with God. (*Lead children to the table, making sure everyone can see.*)

Who knows what these dishes are set up for? (*Listen to answers.*) Yes, they are set up for an important part of worship we call communion, or the Lord's Supper. During communion, we act out the supper that Jesus had with his disciples just before he died. The minister tells everyone what happened that night and repeats the words that Jesus said, like this (*describe the liturgy followed in your own church*):

"On the night of his arrest, Jesus had dinner with his disciples. He picked up the bread, said grace, and broke the bread into pieces (*break bread*) saying, 'Take, eat. This is my body which is broken for you. Do this remembering me.'" Next, little pieces of bread are passed around, and each person in the congregation takes one and eats it, just as the disciples did when they ate with Jesus.

Then the minister says, "In the same way, he picked up the cup after supper (*raise cup*) and said, 'This is my blood, shed for you. Drink it remembering me.'" Little cups of juice or wine are passed around on trays like these. (*Point out tray.*) We each take one and drink it, just like the disciples drank from Jesus' cup during the Last Supper. Then the minister says a prayer thanking God for the gift of communion.

Churches everywhere celebrate communion. It is one of the two most important and special ways we worship God. The other one is baptism. Communion and baptism are so important that we have a name for them. They are called sacraments.

Celebrating communion brings us closer together as God's people. Just as meals on holidays such as Thanksgiving or Christmas might be times your family comes together and grows even closer as a family, communion brings God's people together and helps us grow closer as the family of God.

Celebrating communion also brings us closer to God. It is a special time, an appointment with the Lord, when we share a taste of bread and juice and remember the love God showed us by sending us Jesus. We remember how Jesus was hurt and killed at the end of his life, how his body was broken and his blood shed. We remember that Jesus went through that pain because he loved God, and he loves us. And we remember that God raised Jesus to new life and promises new life to each of us too.

In our church, anyone who has been baptized and loves Jesus is welcome to eat the bread and drink the juice during communion. Some parents want their small children to wait until they're a little older and understand it a little better before they take communion. Talk it over with your parents when you get home, and see what they say. (*If children are present in worship during communion, explain your church's policy concerning their participation.*) In the meantime, we'll all look forward to our next special appointment with God.

Let's Pray. Dear God, we know you are with us all the time, and we can talk with you whenever we want. We thank you also for the special appointments we share with you, the sacraments. In Jesus' name. Amen.

The Wisdom of Solomon

Props and Preparation Needed

Two big dolls and two small dolls. Tie a red ribbon on the wrist of one big doll and one small doll, and a blue ribbon on the other dolls' wrists

A picture of Solomon's temple (may be found in church school curriculum)

The Message

A few weeks ago, we talked about Israel's greatest king. Do you remember his name? (*Listen to answers.*) King David, that's right. The bible says that David was king of Israel for forty years. Before he died, David chose his son Solomon to take his place as king.

One night, Solomon dreamed that the Lord asked him, "What gift would you like me to give to you?" Solomon thought about it and decided that to be a really good king, he would need to be very wise and understand right and wrong, so he asked God for wisdom. The Lord was pleased by Solomon's wish and promised that if he obeyed God, like his father David had, Solomon would be the wisest man in the world. And because his wish for wisdom was such a good choice, God also promised Solomon riches, the respect of other people, and a long life.

One time Solomon proved how wise he was when two women came to him with a problem. (*Use dolls to illustrate.*) The red woman told the king that she and the blue woman lived in the same house. (*Hold up big dolls.*) Each woman had a baby. (*Put babies with mothers according to ribbon colors.*) The red woman said that the blue mother's baby had died in the middle of the night. (*Take away blue baby.*) When she found her child dead, she stole the red mother's baby (*put red baby with blue mother*) and put her dead baby in its place. (*Put blue baby with red mother.*) The red mother told the king, "But I could tell the dead baby was not mine, and I want you to make her give me my living baby back."

Of course the blue mother, whose real baby had died, said that the red mother was lying. Solomon had to decide who was telling the truth. What would you do if you were King Solomon? How would you figure out who was the real mother? (*Pause for answers.*)

The king said, "Bring me a sword." A servant brought a sword. Then the king said, "Cut the living baby in two, and give one half to one mother and the other half to the other mother." But the red mother said to the king, "No, please, don't! Give her the living baby, but please, don't kill him!" The blue mother said to go ahead and cut the baby in two so that neither one of them could have it. Then King Solomon said, "Give the baby to the red woman. She is its real mother." He knew that the baby's real mother would rather give him up to someone else than see him hurt.

Solomon was a wise king. He was also a busy king. His father David had been busy fighting wars, but Israel was at peace when Solomon was king. This gave Solomon time for other things—like building projects. The most important building built while Solomon was king was the temple. (*Show picture.*) This is what the temple looked like. The temple was in Jerusalem, and God's people came from all over Israel to worship there. Jesus and the disciples worshipped at the temple many times, and it is written about over and over again in the Bible. When we read about the temple in Jerusalem, it is the temple that Solomon had built.

Let's Pray. Dear God, may we be wise and productive like Solomon, and may we always be your faithful servants. Amen.

Come, Labor On

Props Needed
Several factory-made toys

The Message
Good morning. School is just about to begin for the year, isn't
it? How many of you will be going to school this week? Are any of
you starting kindergarten? Are you looking forward to going to
kindergarten? I think you'll really like it. (*Of course you'll need to
adjust this opening conversation if the school schedule is different
in your area. For example: How was your first week of school?*)
   Before school begins, we have one more holiday, and it's tomorrow. Does anyone know what holiday that is? (*Listen to answers.*)
Tomorrow is Labor Day, that's right. Labor is another word for
hard work, and Labor Day is a holiday to honor the workers of
our country.
   I have several things to show you this morning. Here is a doll,
a metal truck, a box of crayons, and a pair of roller skates. All of
these toys have something in common. Can you guess what that
is? (*Pause.*) Yes, they are all toys, and they're all fun to play with.
And they were also all made in factories. Factories are huge
buildings with lots of machines and people in them, people who
make things like these toys. Many things are made in factories—
toys, cars, clothes, shoes, food that comes in cans or boxes, pencils, furniture, and lots of other things.
   The first Labor Day was celebrated in the state of New York in
1882—more than one hundred years ago—to thank the people
who worked in factories for all the hard labor they did during the
year. Because, without workers to make and build things, we
wouldn't have much of a country, would we?
   Today most people who work—whether their jobs are in factories, in offices, or outdoors—have the day off for Labor Day. Many
people have picnics or barbecues to celebrate Labor Day. Are any
of you going to a picnic or a barbecue tomorrow?

Grownups have their work, and children have work too. Many of you have the job of going to school, and learning is your job. Your work is school work. If you are too young to be in school, then playing is your work, because you learn all kinds of important things about the world and your place in it when you play.

So grownups have work to do, and children have work to do. All of us also have important work to do as Christians. God has given us the job of helping to take care of God's people. If someone is hungry or sick or lonely or sad, it is our job as Christians to help that person in any way we can. Because we love God, we also love God's people and want to help them when they need it.

When you cheer up a sad friend, send a get-well card to someone who is sick, or visit someone who lives alone, you are not only being a nice person, you are also doing your job. So, happy Labor Day to you.

Let's Pray. Dear God, you have given us an important job to do as Christians. May all of our work be done with love and caring for your people, our brothers and sisters in Christ. Amen.

Church Talk

Props Needed

Pictures of various churches clipped from magazines and mounted on construction paper, file folders, or one large piece of poster board

The Message

Good morning, girls and boys. Today we're going to talk about the church. What do you think about when I say church? (*Listen to answers.*) Most of us think of church as a place we come to be together to worship and learn about God. When we say we're "going to church," we mean this building. We may have friends who go to other churches—different buildings where they go to worship and learn about God.

Here are some pictures of churches. (*Line pictures up so children can see all of them at once.*) How are these churches different from one another? (*Listen to answers.*) In what ways are these churches the same? (*Listen.*)

Church buildings are different in many ways, but one thing that makes all churches the same is the people. Christian people learning about, worshipping, and serving God together is what makes us the church. This building isn't the church. We are. The same is true for all churches everywhere. It's God's people that make any building a church.

If our church burned down, we would still be the Presbyterian Church of Abilene, even if we met in a high school auditorium, a movie theater, or a baseball stadium. Some small churches don't have buildings at all. They meet in the church members' homes each Sunday. You and I and everyone here—we are the church, not the walls, the roof, the floor, and the seats. This building is very nice to have. It is beautiful and gives us a place to meet which helps us remember God, but the people here are the church, not the building.

One way we use the word church is to talk about all the people in all the separate churches around town and around the world—the people in our church, our Methodist friends who are the church down the street, Christians in churches in California and Florida, Mexico and Canada, Africa and Europe. There are thousands and thousands of churches in the world.

Another way we use the word church is to talk about all those people from all those separate churches together as one community of faith. All Christians everywhere, including you and me, make up Christ's church.

It's like a family. You have people who live in the same house as you, right? Those people are your family. You probably also have some aunts, uncles, cousins, and grandparents who don't live in the same house as you. They live in their own houses or apartments, but they are still part of your family. I have some cousins I've never even met, but they are still my family.

We worship together here, and the Methodist Church worships down the street, and Christians worship in different places all around the globe. But we are all part of the same family. We, together, are the church.

Let's Pray. Dear God, we thank you for our church family that meets right here in this building every week, and we thank you for making us part of something much bigger—the church universal, Christ's church. In Jesus' name. Amen.

Thinking and Speaking

Props and Preparation Needed

A hand puppet and puppeteer (see Seventh Sunday after Pentecost, Proper 9, for details)

The Message

Hi, everybody. You may remember my friend, Jack Rabbit. He's here with us again this morning. Come out and say hello to the children, Jack.

Puppet (P):   Hello, children. Hello, Pastor Dianne.

Storyteller (ST):   Hi Jack. I haven't seen you in a long time.

P: I know. What have you done to your hair? It looks like your barber cut it with a lawnmower. Ha, ha! Just kidding. What are y'all doing?

ST: We're having our time together like we do each Sunday morning.

P: Oh, good! I'm a little sleepy. Maybe I can take a quick nap while you tell one of your boring stores. Ha, ha! Just kidding. What're you talking about today?

ST: Well, actually, this is a good week for you to be here. We're going to talk about not hurting each other's feelings with the things we say.

P: Oh, I know what you mean. Just last week I was playing basketball with my friend, Peter. I was having trouble getting the ball through the hoop to make a basket. It's really hard, and I haven't been playing basketball for very long. Well, Peter, who is very tall for a rabbit, said I couldn't score a basket because I was a shrimp and a klutz.

ST: How did that make you feel when your friend called you mean names?

P: Really sad. I didn't want to play with him any more after that, so I went home. But then there was no one else to play with, so I was sad, lonely, and bored. And it was all Peter's fault. Saying mean things to other people is a rotten thing to do.

ST: Do you really think so?

P: Of course I do. Don't you?

ST: Yes, I do. But if you think that saying mean things is rotten, why did you make those cracks about my hair being cut with a lawnmower and my stories being boring?

P: Oh, but I told you I was only kidding.

ST: You know, Jack, saying something mean and then adding "Oh, I'm just kidding" afterwards can hurt a person's feelings too. If Peter had said that he was only kidding after calling you a shrimp and a klutz, would you have liked being called those names?

P: It might not have hurt my feelings quite so bad, but it still would have hurt a little.

ST: That's right. Saying that you're "only kidding" or "just joking" after insulting someone doesn't automatically erase the insult. The person still hears the mean words, and they still hurt. The same is true with "sorry." If we hurt a friend's feelings, of course we need to say we're sorry. But we can't go around saying whatever we want to say without thinking about other people's feelings, and then expect "sorry" to magically take care of any hurt feelings our words may have caused. Once we say something, we can never take it back. It's been said—and heard. There's no way to unsay or unhear the words once they're out of our mouths.

P: That means we really have to think about what we say before we say it, doesn't it, so we won't blurt out something mean or thoughtless.

ST: That's a good way to put it.

P: Oh, Pastor Dianne, I am sorry if I hurt your feelings earlier. I really do like your stories.

ST: Thank you, Jack. And what about my hair?

P: Don't ask. I'm sorry I brought it up.

Let's Pray. Dear God, help us to be considerate of the feelings of others in what we say and do. Help us to think before we speak and to forgive others when they fail to consider us. Amen.

EIGHTEENTH SUNDAY AFTER   Proper 20
PENTECOST   Servanthood
Mark 9:30–37

Where Is the Front?

Props Needed

Lollipops, cookies, or some other appealing treats—one for each child

The Message

I brought some treats to share with you this morning. I hope I brought enough for everyone. Who would like a treat? Who would like to be first? Okay, line up and I'll pass them out. (*Wait for children to line up. Walk toward the front of the line, but then bypass the first child, and walk to the end of the line. Pass out the treats, beginning with the last child and ending with the first.*)

Did everyone get a lollipop? Okay, let's go back over and sit down together. When you first lined up, how did those in the back of the line feel? (*Listen to answers.*) How did those in the front of the line feel? (*Listen.*) What did the first people in line think when I walked right past you and began handing out treats at the end of the line? (*Listen.*) And those at the end, how did you feel when I gave the treats to you first? (*Listen.*)

Jesus taught his disciples that if they wanted to be really great, then they needed to be last, because truly great people are those who care about the needs of others before their own needs. Jesus taught his disciples to be servants, to take care of other people without worrying about getting credit or reward. Jesus taught that the most humble people will be the most respected and honored on God's Earth.

Does anybody know what it means to be humble? We sometimes think of humble as the opposite of conceited. Being conceited is when you think you're better than everybody else. Sometimes we think that being humble means thinking that everyone else is better than you are, but that isn't really true. Being humble means choosing to put the needs of others before your own. It is choosing to care for others—not because they're better than you, but because you love them.

Jesus is the best example of a truly humble person. Jesus chose to leave heaven and come to Earth to show us the way to God, even though living on Earth was painful and hard compared to heaven. He chose to come and teach and suffer—and even die—on Earth because he loves us. The needs of God's people for love and forgiveness were more important to Jesus than his own needs, so he came to Earth as a humble servant. He taught his disciples to be humble servants too.

We, too, are Jesus' followers, his modern-day disciples. We need to follow Jesus' example and be humble servants of God by helping others. Some people will tell you that this idea is nuts. They will say that everyone needs to look out for number one and grab all he or she can get without worrying about the other guy having enough. Jesus said that this selfish way of living is all wrong and that those who choose the front of the line in this life will be at the back of the line in heaven.

Let's Pray. Dear God, we thank you that Jesus loved us enough to give up all he had to come and live among us. Help us to follow his example, and live a life of humble service. In Jesus' name. Amen.

A Gift from God

Props Needed
An eight- to twelve-inch ribbon for each child

The Message
How many of you like to get presents? For my sixth birthday, I got a red bicycle with training wheels and a horn. That was one of my favorite presents of all time. (*Use your own example.*) What is the best present you ever received? (*Listen to answers.*)

People give each other presents for special occasions like birthdays and Christmas, or when someone is sick or sad and needs cheering up, or sometimes just to show that they love one another. God gives presents, too, to show how much God loves us. Can you think of some of the gifts God gives us? (*Listen to answers.*) Yes, God gives us the Earth, the plants and animals, food to eat, and families that love us. One of the most precious gifts God gives to us is you. Children are one of God's most important and special gifts.

God gives children to the grownups in the world to love and care for until the children are grownups themselves. God expects grownups to cherish this gift, to make all children feel special and keep all children safe.

Most adults understand what a wonderful gift children are and try their best to be good to all boys and girls, whether as parents, grandparents, aunts, uncles, cousins, neighbors, or friends. But there are some grownups who do not understand how God wants children to be treated. There are some people who hurt children on purpose, and this is very, very bad.

Now I'm not talking about when your mom or dad gives you a spanking on the bottom to teach you a lesson because you've done something wrong. I'm talking about a different and more serious kind of hurt, a kind of hurt that makes you feel bad about yourself, even if you haven't done anything wrong.

If anyone ever touches you in a way that makes you feel uncomfortable, or if anyone ever tries to get you to play touching or tickling games that make you feel icky inside, tell that person no, and then tell a grownup you trust what happened. If it's a stranger, or even someone you know, who tries to touch you or wants you to touch them in ways you don't like, it's okay to say no. Then be sure to tell a grownup you trust about what happened, even if the bad grownup warns you not to tell anyone, or threatens to hurt you or your family if you tell. The grownups you trust will protect you from the bad person. And if the first person you tell doesn't believe you, then tell someone else—your parents, your teachers, me—until someone does believe you.

It's very sad that we cannot trust all people to treat children with the tenderness and care they deserve, but we can't. That's why you should never talk to a stranger, never get into a stranger's car, and let your parents know where you are all the time. But to help you and everyone who sees you today remember what a precious gift you are, I have a ribbon to tie around your wrist. (*Tie a ribbon around each child's wrist.*)

Let's Pray. Dear God, we thank you for these children, the most precious of your gifts. Help all of us to cherish, nurture, and protect them. Amen.

TWENTIETH SUNDAY AFTER   Proper 22
PENTECOST   Caring for Creation
Psalm 8

Endangered

Prop Needed
A plastic dinosaur

The Message
Who can tell me what kind of dinosaur this is? (*Show prop.*) A stegosaurus, that's right. How did you know this was a stegosaurus? (*Pause.*) By the bony plates on its back. Very good.

Dinosaurs are very interesting and even mysterious animals, aren't they? We know a lot about dinosaurs—where they lived, how big they were, and what they ate. But there are many things we may never know about dinosaurs—like what colors they were—because there are no dinosaurs living today. They are extinct. When all of a certain kind of animal dies, like all the dinosaurs have died, then we call that animal extinct. Once an animal is extinct, it is gone forever. We can never get it back again.

There are many, many animals in our world that are not extinct yet but are in danger of dying out and becoming extinct. We call these endangered animals. Cheetahs, elephants, gorillas, leopards, otters, rhinoceros, tigers, gray wolves, humpback whales, mountain zebras, American bald eagles, alligators, and crocodiles are all endangered animals.

We don't really know why all the dinosaurs died and became extinct, but we do know what is killing so many of these other animals that they are endangered. In one way or another, these animals are being killed by people, and there are more of these animals dying than there are being born.

Some animals are killed by hunters because people want some part of the animal. Animals such as leopards and otters are killed for their fur, to make coats. Elephants are killed for their tusks, to make ivory jewelry or carvings. And alligators are killed for their skins, to make shoes and purses. It is illegal to kill these animals because they are endangered, but people will pay a lot of money for a leopard-fur coat or a pair of alligator shoes, so some hunters are willing to break the law and risk getting caught. These hunters are called poachers.

Other animals are killed because people are afraid of them. Wolves have been misunderstood for years and years. Some people are afraid of being attacked by wolves, so whenever they see a wolf, they shoot it, whether that particular wolf is really dangerous or not.

Many types of animals are endangered because their homes have been taken away. Land that used to be wild grassland or rain forest has been turned into farmland for crops. And as cities and towns grow, wild land is cleared to make room for more people. Houses, stores, schools, roads—even churches—now stand where tigers once hunted and elephants once grazed. When people move in, there isn't as much room or food for the animals, so they starve.

Many people are worried about losing endangered animals forever. Many people are working to save animals from becoming extinct like the dinosaurs did because those people know that God gave us this planet and all of its creatures. Earth and everything on it are gifts for us to take care of, not to destroy. You can help take care of the Earth by recycling, not wasting water, walking or riding your bike whenever you can, turning off lights when you don't need them, handing down clothes and toys to younger children when you're finished with them, growing some of your own food, only buying things you really need, planting trees, and making sure never to buy things made from endangered animals or rain forest trees. When you go home today, talk with your parents about ways your family can help take care of God's gift, planet Earth.

Let's Pray. Dear God, we thank you for our earthly home. Help us make our planet a safe and happy home for all your creatures. Amen.

TWENTY-FIRST SUNDAY AFTER   Proper 23
PENTECOST   Reign of God
Mark 10:17–31

Sewing Up Salvation

Props Needed

A needle with a medium-sized eye
A piece of thread
A piece of yarn

The Message

Do any of you know how to sew? Do any of you know how to thread a needle? I have a needle and thread here. Sarah, would you like to try and thread the needle? (*Give one child the needle and thread.*) Every needle has a hole at the top of it called the eye. Sarah is going to put the thread through the eye of the needle. There, she did it! Good job, Sarah. Now the needle and thread are ready to be used for sewing on a button, patching some jeans, or hemming a skirt.

Was it easy or hard to get the thread through the eye of the needle, Sara? (*Listen to answer.*) What if you were to try and get this piece of yarn through the needle's eye—would that be easy or hard? (*Listen.*) What about Mrs. Olson over there? Would it be easy or hard to get Mrs. Olson through the eye of that needle?

One time when Jesus was just starting out on a trip, a man rushed over, knelt down, and asked, "Good Teacher, what must I do to go to heaven?" Jesus could tell the man was trying to impress him by kneeling and calling him "Good Teacher," but he answered the man's question anyway. He told the man to obey God's Law, to follow the Ten Commandments. The man said that he had obeyed the Law since he was a child.

Jesus looked at the man and felt great love for him. Then Jesus told the man, "You are missing one thing, go, sell everything you own, and give the money to the poor, and you will have treasure in heaven; then come, follow me." When the man heard Jesus' answer, he was shocked and went away sadly because he was rich.

As the man walked away with his head bent down, Jesus turned to his disciples and said, "It is very hard for a rich person to enter the Reign of God, or heaven." Then he said, "It is easier for a camel to go through the eye of a needle than for a rich person to enter the Reign of God."

The disciples thought this was a very odd thing to say, but the rich man had proven Jesus' point very well. We all get attached to our things. I'm sure you like all the things that are in your toy boxes and closets. The things that are yours alone mean a lot to you. That is okay. But it is not okay when our things become more important to us than anything else in our lives, such as our family, our friends, or God. The rich man loved God. He proved that by obeying God's law. But he loved his things more, since he would not sell them, give away the money, and follow Jesus— even when the reward for doing it was living in God's realm.

The disciples asked Jesus, "Well, if the rich can't even buy their way into heaven, then who will be in God's realm?" Jesus answered them, "For people, heaven is impossible. But for God, all things are possible." If we put our trust in God and not in our things, we too can be a part of God's realm.

Let's Pray. Dear God, we know that all of the good things in our lives come from you. May we never make the gift more important than the giver. In Jesus' name. Amen.

TWENTY-SECOND SUNDAY   Proper 24
AFTER PENTECOST   Church Community/Talents
Mark 10:35–45

The Blue Community

Prop Needed

A toy Smurf figure or something that has a picture of a Smurf character on it

The Message

Have you ever seen "The Smurfs" cartoon show on television? For those who haven't, the Smurfs are little blue people who live in a Smurf village in a forest. They look like this. (*Show prop.*) Each Smurf has a special talent, a thing that Smurf does especially well.

Baker Smurf cooks up delicious treats for all the members of the village to enjoy. Handyman Smurf is especially good at fixing things that are broken. There is a farmer Smurf, an artist Smurf, a Smurf poet, and Smurf children. The leader of the village is the oldest and wisest Smurf of all. Do you know his name? (*Pause.*) Papa Smurf, that's right. Papa Smurf is like everybody's mayor, teacher, and grandfather all rolled up in one. He leads the community of Smurfs wisely, fairly, and with love.

Now each Smurf is different, which is a good thing. They all work together, sharing their talents with each other to make their village a happy place. Can you imagine what would happen if all the Smurfs were poets? Who would fix the things that broke? Or if all the Smurfs were like Papa Smurf, who would grow the crops or paint the pretty pictures? Each Smurf is different, and each Smurf is just as important as the others. Even Papa Smurf couldn't get along alone, without all of the other Smurfs' talents. It is only by working together and sharing with each other that the Smurf village can survive. We call working together and sharing with each other "community." The Smurfs live together in community with each other.

The church community is a lot like the Smurf community. Everybody in the church is good at something. Some of us are good

122

teachers, and some are good students. Others are good singers, good ushers, or good listeners. Some of us are good at handling the church's money, and some are good at cheering up people who are sad or lonely. Some of us have very good ideas, while others are good at crafts, or at holding babies, or at letting other people know we like them. Some of us are good preachers, while others are good acolytes—or even good smilers. God has given each one of us something that we do especially well so that we can share that talent with the rest of the church community.

If all of us were good preachers, then who would be here to listen? If we all wanted to be ushers, then who would we take to the seats? If we were all good eaters, but none of us could cook, we would really have a problem, wouldn't we?

God gives each of us a talent. By working together and sharing our talents with each other, we build a strong community of faith. That community is the church.

Let's Pray. Thank you, God, for the many amazing talents you have given our community of faith through its members. May we be generous in sharing our time and talents with each other. Amen.

Spooky Spooks and Ghoulish Goblins

Prop Needed
A scary Halloween mask

The Message
Are you all looking forward to Halloween? What costumes are you going to wear? (*Listen to answers.*) Those sound like some terrific costumes! Some people like to look as scary as they can on Halloween. They might wear raggedy clothes, pour some fake blood on themselves, and wear an ugly mask like this one. (*Put prop up to your face for a couple of seconds.*) When you go to a Halloween party or out trick-or-treating, are you ever frightened by some of the costumes you see? (*Pause.*) Very young children are sometimes afraid because they don't understand (*put up mask*) that there is a person (*take down mask*) behind the scary face. But most of you know that the costumes people wear for Halloween are make-believe. The people behind those masks are your friends and neighbors, brothers and sisters—maybe even your minister. So you don't need to be afraid of Halloween, unless you want to be—like going through a haunted house, when it's fun to be afraid.

There are other things in life that do frighten us, though. Have you ever been lost in a shopping mall, at a ball game, or in the woods? Being lost can be very frightening. Sometimes we may hear our parents arguing loudly, or we may get yelled at for doing something wrong. Trying something new like skiing or swimming, or taking a test we haven't studied for can also be scary experiences. Moving to a new town or having to speak in front of a crowd can be scary if you're shy.

All of these things can be scary if we let them, but they don't have to be. There is a poem in the Bible in which the author wrote about walking through the valley of the shadow of death. That sounds like a pretty scary place, doesn't it? But he said that, even if he walked through the valley of the shadow of death, he would not be afraid because he knew that God was with him.

God is with us everywhere, no matter what is happening. If we're lost or alone or being yelled at, or if we're the only new kid on the block—God is with us. We do not ever have to be afraid. We are never alone. And if you feel afraid sometimes, even though you know God is with you, talk to God. Pray, and you will feel better and stronger.

Let's Pray. Dear God, thank you for always being with us. Help us to trust you and to know that together with the helpers you send our way, like our parents and teachers and friends, we can beat any challenge we face. Amen.

TWENTY-FOURTH SUNDAY AFTER   Proper 26
PENTECOST   Ruth and Naomi
Ruth 1:1–18

Your People Shall Be My People

Prop Needed
A passport

The Message
I have something interesting to show you this morning. (*Hold up prop.*) It's a passport. If you were going on a trip to a foreign country—like England or Japan—you would have to take your passport with you. A passport lists your name and address (*show these sections as you mention them*), has your picture in it, and—most important of all—proves that you are a citizen of the United States. When you visit another country, or even if you live there, you are still a citizen of the country in which you were born, and you need a passport from that country to prove it.

Our story this morning begins with Naomi, a woman from Israel, and her husband, Elimelech, who went with their two sons to live in a foreign country. There was a famine in Israel, which means there wasn't enough food to go around, so Naomi's family moved to the country of Moab. While they lived there, the sons met and married two women from Moab, Orpah and Ruth. Then Elimelech and his two sons died, and the three women were all left without husbands. Suddenly, they were all widows.

Losing a husband and becoming a widow today is very hard, but it was even harder during the time of our story, thousands of years ago. Women were not allowed to have jobs, and Naomi, Orpah, and Ruth had no money. Their best chance was to go home to their parents' houses or to get married again. Otherwise they might starve.

Not knowing what else to do, Naomi decided to go home to Bethlehem, which is in Israel, and Orpah and Ruth started the trip with her. They hadn't gone far, though, when Naomi told the other two that they should stay in Moab and go home to their own villages, where they might be able to find new husbands. Orpah was sad as she left for home.

Ruth loved Naomi too much to leave her and begged to be allowed to stay with Naomi. Ruth said, "Wherever you go, I will go. Wherever you sleep, I will sleep. Your people shall be my people, and your God shall be my God." Naomi loved Ruth, too, and agreed to let her come along.

In Israel, people were supposed to be kind to widows. For example, after crops were harvested, farmers allowed widows to look in the fields for food the farmers' helpers may have missed. It was called gleaning the fields.

One day Ruth was gleaning the fields of a rich farmer named Boaz. Boaz noticed Ruth and had his farm hands leave extra grain behind for her to find. Boaz was very kind to Ruth, and she loved him in return. After a while, they got married and had a baby boy. Naomi was honored as the boy's grandmother and also became his babysitter. The baby's name was Obed, and he later became the grandfather of the greatest king of Israel, King David.

Let's Pray. Dear God, we thank you for the gifts of family and friendship. We thank you for the special blessing of when those in our family are also our friends. Amen.

TWENTY-FIFTH SUNDAY AFTER   Proper 27
PENTECOST   Elijah
1 Kings 17:8–16

Free Refills

Props Needed

A Pez candy dispenser filled with candies and enough refills so that each child gets a piece

The Message

I have something with me this morning that many of you have probably seen before. Who knows what this is? (*Hold up prop.*) A Pez dispenser, that's right.

This one has a Snoopy head on top. What happens when you tip Snoopy's head back? (*Tip the head back.*) A candy pops out. Would anyone like a piece? (*Give everyone a piece of candy. When the candy is gone, say, "Oh look, it ran out. I'll have to refill it." Then continue distributing candy until everyone has a piece.*)

Did everyone get a piece of candy? Good, because Snoopy is almost empty again, and I don't have any more refills to put in it. Wouldn't it be great if someone could invent a candy dispenser that never, ever ran out of candy? It would never be empty. Every time you felt like eating a piece of candy, one would be there, no matter how many times you tipped Snoopy's head back. Well, our story this morning has something like that happen in it. The story comes from the Old Testament of the Bible, which means it happened before Jesus was born. It is about one of God's prophets, Elijah, and a poor woman who helped him.

The king of Israel at this time was named Ahab. He was a wicked king who worshipped a fake God named Baal and even built an altar to him. Because the king turned away from the Lord to worship the pretend God, many of the people of Israel did too. This made the Lord sad and angry, because he knew that Baal could never help the people—Baal wasn't real. Only the Lord God of Israel could answer the people's prayers. God had to find a way to show the people how wrong they were to ignore the real God and worship a fake one. So the Lord did a simple thing. The Lord stopped sending rain.

Every living thing needs water to survive—plants, animals, and people. At first there was enough water in the rivers and lakes to keep the plants, animals, and people alive. But with no rain to refill them, the rivers and lakes began to dry up. The people started running out of food because there was no rain to water their crops for three years.

God had a prophet named Elijah. The Lord had plans for Elijah when it came time to end the drought and send the rain again, but it wasn't time yet. The Lord wanted to keep Elijah safe until it was time, so God told Elijah that a poor widow—a woman whose husband was dead—would feed him until he was needed. Elijah went to the city of Zarephath, as God told him to, and he saw the widow outside the city gates collecting sticks.

Elijah asked her for a drink, which she brought him. Then he asked her for some bread to eat. She looked very tired and sad and said, "I have nothing baked. All I have is a small handful of meal in a jar and a tiny bit of oil in a jug to make some flat cakes. I am gathering sticks to build a fire now. I will make the cakes for my son and me and then, because we have no more food and no way to get more, we will starve."

Elijah told the widow not to be afraid. He told her to go ahead and make the cakes, which were like tortillas, but to give him one first. Then he told her that God would keep her jar of meal and her jug of oil full until it rained again in Israel. And that's what happened. Every day when the widow went to her kitchen to cook breakfast, she found enough meal in the jar and enough oil in the jug to make cakes for Elijah, her son, and herself. The same thing happened at lunch and at supper. God took care of the widow, her son, and their special guest until God proved to the people of Israel that the Lord God was the one who cared for them always by sending rain once again.

Let's Pray. Dear God, thank you for caring for us always. In Jesus' name. Amen.

TWENTY-SIXTH SUNDAY AFTER   Proper 28
PENTECOST   Love
Psalm 116

Sharing Love

Prop Needed
A drawing made by a child and given as a gift to someone he or she loves

The Message
Think of someone you love a whole lot—maybe your mom or dad, or grandparent, brother, sister, or dog. It doesn't matter who—just somebody you love very much. Do you have someone in mind? Okay, remember that person.

I want to show you something that Graham drew for his mother. (*Show prop.*) When he gave it to her, he said, "This is for you, Mom, because I love you." What are some of the ways you show the person you are thinking about that you love him or her? (*Listen to answers.*)

Sharing your artwork, giving hugs and kisses, saying "I love you," taking time to play with someone, helping to clean out the garage, setting the supper table, sending a card or letter if your special person lives in another town, sharing your toys, remembering your special person's birthday, doing what she or he wants to do when you'd rather do something different, being cooperative—all these are good ways to show someone special that you love him or her.

When was the last time you showed your love for your special person? We often want to show the special people in our lives that we love them, don't we? Of course we can't spend all of our time drawing pictures to give away and sharing hugs and kisses. Saying "Mommy, I love you" twenty thousand times a day would even get old after awhile. The best way to show your love for someone is to be the most terrific son or daughter, grandchild, sister, brother, friend, student, or neighbor that you can be.

The same thing is true with God. There are many ways we can show our love for God. We can pray and tell God of our love. We can come to worship God. We can sing songs that say how much we love God. But the very best way to show God our love is to be the best person we can be. Part of being the best person we can be is to be kind and generous to other people; when we treat others well, then we are also showing how much we love God.

If a friend said, "I really like you. I'm so glad we're friends," that would make you feel pretty good, wouldn't it? But if your friend said, "I really like you," and then broke your favorite toy on purpose, or said mean things about you to others behind your back, or kicked your dog, it would be hard to believe she meant what she said about liking you, wouldn't it? That's what I'm talking about. The best way to show our love for someone is to do our best to be a kind, generous, loving, faithful person ourselves.

Let's Pray. Dear God, you have given us many people who love us and special folks for us to love in return. Help us to show our love by being the best children of God we can be. Amen.

Turkey Talk

Props and Preparation Needed
Flannel board
Flannel-board turkey (found in the Appendix). Copy the turkey
head and body onto brown construction paper and cut it out. Using the feather pattern as a guide, cut ten or twelve feathers from
construction paper of various colors. Prepare turkey and feathers
for use on flannel board
A black felt-tipped marker

The Message
What do corn, native Americans, Pilgrims, turkey, the Mayflower, and God have in common? (*Pause for answers.*) That's
right, all those things are a part of the Thanksgiving story. This
Thursday is Thanksgiving, so this would be a perfect time to tell
the story of the first Thanksgiving again.

The story begins in the country of England, which is clear
across the Atlantic Ocean from here. It was summer, more than
three hundred years ago, when a small ship called the Mayflower
was loaded with supplies and one hundred and two passengers,
many of them children. Then the Mayflower set sail from England to the New World across the ocean. The people were coming
to America, but it wasn't called America yet. America was a huge
land with no stores, no roads, and not many people. The people
who lived here, the native Americans, had lived here a long time,
and very few of them spoke English.

The Pilgrims on board the Mayflower probably wondered what
the people on the warm, sunny coast of Virginia would be like.

The trip took many months. When the Pilgrims finally spotted
land in the distance, it wasn't summer any more, but winter. And
the land they saw wasn't sunny, warm Virginia. It was cold,
snowy Massachusetts. A storm had blown them off course, and
they were in the wrong place. But it would be too hard to sail
down the coast to where it was warm, so the Pilgrims decided to
make a home for themselves where they were.

That first winter in the New World was very hard for the Pilgrims. Many people had died on the ship during their voyage, and more people died in the bitter cold of Massachusetts. Finally spring came, and things began to look better. The Pilgrims built small wooden homes and slowly made friends with the native Americans, who taught them how to plant corn by putting a small fish in the hole with each seed. The fish acted as fertilizer and helped the seeds grow. The Pilgrims picked the wild fruit and nuts that grew in the warmer weather to eat with the animals they hunted for meat. And when it came time to harvest the corn, there was a very big crop that would help them better survive the next winter.

The Pilgrims decided to set aside a special day to thank God for their good crops and all the blessings they enjoyed in their new home. They invited their new friends, the native Americans, to come to a feast and to join them in thanksgiving. Ninety native Americans came and stayed three days. It was a happy celebration, and there was enough food and fun for everyone.

The Pilgrims knew that all the good things in their lives—the corn, the babies, the new friends, the new homes, the animals to hunt and fish to catch for food, their families—all the good things in their lives came from God, and God deserved their thanks. Giving thanks is what Thanksgiving is still about today.

Think about all of the good things in your life. Mr. Turkey here is going to help us thank God for those good things. (*Put turkey on the flannel board.*) Out of all the good things in your life, tell me the ones for which you are especially thankful this year. Ryan, what are you thankful for? (*If children are slow to respond, give your own example first. As they offer answers, write each one on a turkey feather, then put the feather on the flannel-board turkey.*)

Let's Pray. Dear God, we know that all good gifts come from you. We give you our honest and heartfelt thanks for these blessings and all the others which fill our lives. In Jesus' name. Amen.

Appendix

How to Prepare Flannel-board Figures

Cut the page containing the needed flannel-board figures out of the book. Glue the page onto a piece of stiff cardboard, such as the cardboard that comes with a new shirt. Cut around the outline of each figure. Color the figures with crayons, marking pens, or colored pencils. Glue small squares of medium-grade sandpaper to the top, bottom, and middle of the back of each figure.

Samuel

Eli

Who Said That?
(pages 24–25)

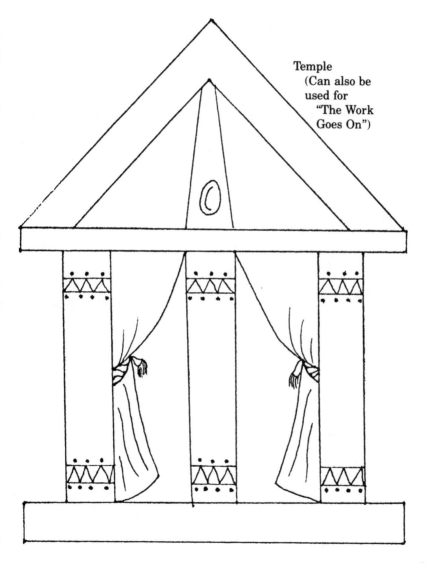

Temple
(Can also be
used for
"The Work
Goes On")

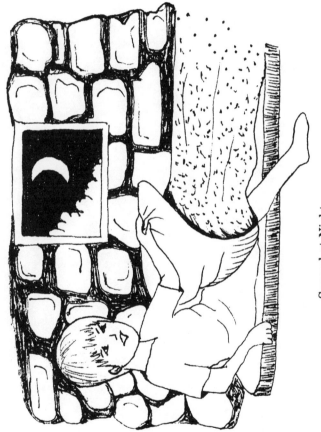

Samuel at Night

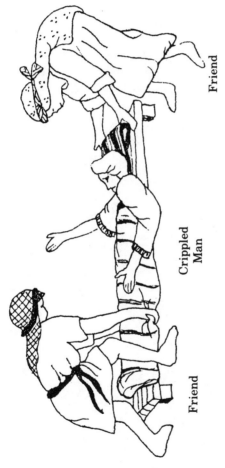

The Work Goes On
(pages 64–65)

Peter & John

Leaping Man

Beautiful Gate

The "In" Crowd
(pages 82–83)

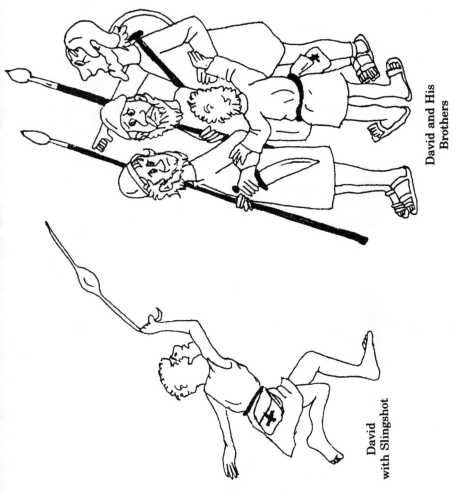

David and His Brothers

David
with Slingshot

The Mighty Fall
(pages 86–87)

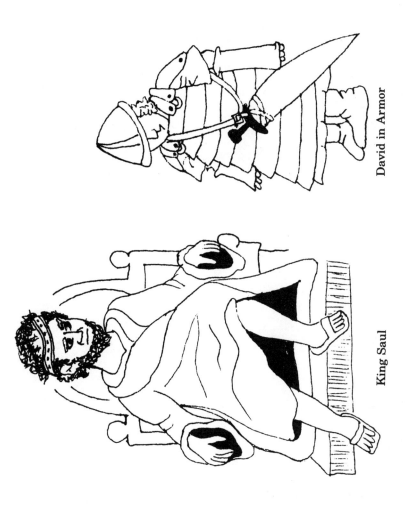

David in Armor

King Saul

Goliath

Jamie

#1 Ordinary Face

#2 Angry Face

Jamie's Answers
(pages 98–99)

Hitting Brother

#3 Hitting Pillow

#4   Excited Face

#6   Sad Face

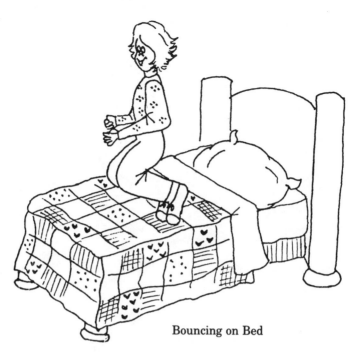

Bouncing on Bed

#5
Doing Cartwheels

163

#7
Hugging
Lion

#8   Happy Face

#9 Dancing-Marching

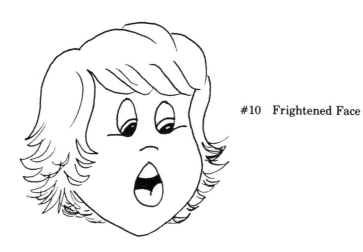

#10 Frightened Face

#11 Hiding under Covers

Hiding in Corner

#12
Hugging

#13
Happy

Turkey

Turkey
Feather

Turkey Talk
(pages 132–133)

How to Make the Flannel Board

Cut a piece of masonite or foam board to the desired size. Using powder-blue flannel four inches larger than the board (Diagram 1), pull the flannel to the back of the board, making sure it is smooth and taut on the front. Glue or tape the corners of the flannel to the back of the board first (Diagram 2). Then glue or tape the top and bottom edges (Diagram 3), and finally the side edges (Diagram 4).

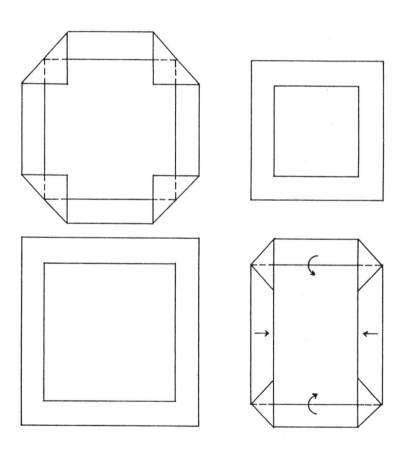

Indexes

Scripture Index

Topical Index